Also by Fay Vincent

The Last Commissioner: A Baseball Valentine

THE
ONLY GAME
IN TOWN

Baseball Stars of the 1930s and 1940s
Talk About the Game They Loved

The Baseball Oral History Project

Volume 1

Fay Vincent

Simon & Schuster

New York   London   Toronto   Sydney

SIMON & SCHUSTER
Rockefeller Center
1230 Avenue of the Americas
New York, NY 10020

A leatherbound signed first edition of this book has been
published by Easton Press.

SIMON & SCHUSTER and colophon are registered trademarks
of Simon & Schuster, Inc.

For information about special discounts for bulk purchases,
please contact Simon & Schuster Special Sales at
1-800-456-6798 or business@simonandschuster.com

Designed by C. Linda Dingler

Manufactured in the United States of America

10   9   8   7   6   5   4   3   2   1

Library of Congress Cataloging-in-Publication Data is available.

ISBN-13: 978-0-7432-7317-6
ISBN-10:   0-7432-7317-6

All photos courtesy of the National Baseball Hall of Fame Library,
Cooperstown, New York, except photos on pp. 68, 116, and 190,
which are courtesy of AP/Wide World Photos.

*To Herbert Allen, George Cooney, and Claire Smith,
whose support and friendship I cherish.*

CONTENTS

vii

THE
ONLY GAME
IN TOWN

INTRODUCTION

SOME TEN YEARS AGO a friend gave me a copy of the audiotapes that were the basis of Lawrence Ritter's book *The Glory of Their Times*. I was enthralled to listen to those old-time ballplayers talk about their experiences in our game around the turn of the twentieth century. Ritter made such a wonderful contribution to my understanding of the game in those days that I thought about emulating him with players from the 1930s and 1940s, who came along after those whom Ritter featured. One day I idly mentioned my idea to my good friend the estimable investment banker and great baseball fan Herbert Allen, who instantly encouraged me and pledged financial support if I would go out and do the interviewing. This book was born of that conversation.

In checking with the National Baseball Hall of Fame, I learned there was no systematic oral history project being supported by that superb organization and so I undertook to fill that void. I was keenly aware that some important figures in the history of the integration of baseball, such as Larry Doby, were growing older and their stories would soon be lost forever. With that as motivation, I began this project. Herbert and I set up a tax-exempt foundation to provide some structure for our work, and we each gave money to support the interviewing and the necessary archival work at the Hall of Fame. (My thanks go to Steve Greenberg, treasurer of the foundation, for handling these financial matters.) We were joined by a third major contributor, George Cooney, whose video company, EUE Screen Gems, has provided gratis the camera crews and technical support to videotape every interview we have done. His help has been extraordinary and our gratitude is every bit as enormous as his generosity.

In the years since we began this project, we have done close to forty interviews, and we have dozens more planned. For this book, we have selected players who were among the oldest of those we interviewed. The focus of this volume is on the integration of the major leagues. We chose interviews with Buck O'Neil and Elden Auker, two remarkable men who played their careers prior to integration, and we include Larry Doby and Monte Irvin to capture the coming of players of color to their rightful place in the game. The stories of Bob Feller, Dom DiMaggio, and Warren Spahn cover the World War II years and remind us of the amount of time those men and other ballplayers lost in their baseball careers by serving their country. Tommy Henrich is one of the few ballplayers alive from those great Yankee teams of the 1930s and 1940s, while Johnny Pesky recalls his years with the Boston Red Sox, playing alongside Ted Williams among others. Ralph Kiner tells of baseball in the glory days right after the war, when integration took hold.

In conducting many of the interviews, including our first one with Larry Doby, I was the partner of the gifted baseball writer Claire Smith, whose contribution to this oral history project cannot be overstated. She has been a thoughtful and wise counselor and I thank her with all my heart. Others have done some interviewing and I thank them as well. They include the late Leonard Koppett, Ed Randall, John Pessah, Mark Hyman, Dick Crago, and James Salisbury.

To put together this book—which I hope will be the first of several volumes of baseball history—I was ably assisted by my Simon & Schuster editor, Bob Bender, who combed the transcripts of the interviews I conducted and arranged the ballplayers' comments into a narrative that I then edited. The Hall of Fame generously provided the photographs in this book, for which I thank Hall of Fame president, Dale Petroskey, and his colleagues Bill Burdick and Pat

Kelly. Additional thanks to Jim Gates at the Hall of Fame. We paid a modest fee to each of the ballplayers whom we interviewed, and by agreement with them, any royalties earned from this book will go to the Hall of Fame, in recognition of its fine work in preserving and disseminating the history of baseball.

In many ways this endeavor has been a labor of love for me. I have enjoyed hearing these great players describe their lives in baseball. In each interview, my first question was always the same: "Who got you interested in baseball? Who gave you your first ball and glove?" Inevitably, the next twenty or so minutes were filled by a delicious conversation. As the interviews grew, I was fascinated to discover that certain key events of the 1930s and 1940s were told—sometimes with small but significant differences—by more than one ballplayer. For example, both Elden Auker and Tommy Henrich tell the story of what happened when Hank Greenberg walked into the Chicago White Sox locker room after a game in which Greenberg had been insulted by anti-Semitic slurs from the White Sox bench. Because Auker was Greenberg's teammate at the time, his is the longer version of this story, but Henrich's account agrees in the key details. Compare Dom DiMaggio's and Johnny Pesky's accounts of Enos Slaughter's famous "dash to home" in Game 7 of the 1946 World Series. Each of them played a key role in that famous event, as you'll see. Warren Spahn tells the story of giving up Willie Mays's first hit on a pitch he was told Mays couldn't hit—but did, for a home run. Monte Irvin, Mays's teammate, tells the story from his vantage point. Everyone, it seems, has at least one Satchel Paige story (or one about Ted Williams or Joe DiMaggio), all of them colorful.

It is my hope that you will enjoy these stories as I do because I am convinced that it is these stories that keep the history of baseball alive.

—Fay Vincent

ELDEN AUKER

Elden Auker was a good pitcher before suffering a shoulder injury in a college football game, but as a result of this unfortunate gridiron moment, a big league star was born. As he describes below, forced to alter his delivery dramatically, from an overhand to an underhanded "submarine" motion, his unique gift—not seen on a major league mound for years—made him the scourge of many batters.

"Auker would come down, and he come from way down under there, and that ball would dive. He'd throw a curve, and it would rise," said infielder Russ Peters. An opposing pitcher, Virgil Trucks, once remarked, "Elden's knuckles used to graze the ground when he delivered the ball."

The right-handed Auker would compile a 130–101 record during his 10-year career (1933–42) spent with the Detroit Tigers, Boston Red Sox, and St. Louis Browns. A consistent starting pitcher, he would win 13 or more games seven times. He would help Detroit to two postseason appearances, losing Game 7 to the St. Louis Cardinals and Dizzy Dean in the 1934 World Series, but helping the team next year defeat the Chicago Cubs in the Fall Classic.

Teammate Firpo Marberry said it was an especially deceptive curve that made Auker a success. "It is not a wide-breaking curve but it's still one of the hardest curveballs to hit that I've seen. Instead of breaking downward, as curveballs nearly always do, Auker's curve breaks upward. Few pitchers have ever been able to make a curveball break upward. And then he has an unorthodox underhand delivery that makes his stuff that much more effective. His curve will cause left-handed batters a great deal of trouble."

A 1934 newspaper story entitled "Auker Baffles Hitters with His Clay Ball" states, *"A clay ball is nothing like the spitter, the screw, the shine, or the forkball. Instead, it is a pitch that starts in the dirt of the pitcher's box and travels with blinding speed to the batter. In addition to his puzzling fastball, Auker has a slow curveball, both thrown underhand after a fashion made famous some dozen or more years ago by Carl Mays, one time a winning Yankee pitcher."*

Though he had won 14 games for the lowly Browns in 1942, Auker would surprise the baseball world by announcing his retirement. Shortly afterward, in a letter to the Detroit News, he explained that there were other challenges he and his country were facing.

"The truth of the matter is that I have been considering giving up baseball for about a year in order to devote my time exclusively to my job in the engineering department of the Midwest Abrasive Co.," Auker wrote. *"The simple truth behind my decision is this: The career of a baseball player is comparatively short and sooner or later it must end. What better time, then, could my baseball career end? What better time, I mean, from the standpoint of my family, my industrial employers, or our country's war effort? Obviously, I am not vain enough to believe for a moment that my work is going to win the war, or that my remaining in baseball will lose it. But I do believe that an attitude different from that, if adopted by too many young men today, can cost us the war."*

MY FATHER WAS A MAIL CARRIER in western Kansas and he was never much interested in sports. The way I got into it was I had an uncle, his name was Frank Brunk. He was a very good athlete, and he was a good baseball player. And when I was in high school, why I started playing catch with him and working with him.

He showed me how to throw a curveball and so on. And the last year in high school, they had a town team, and I ended up

Elden Auker

pitching in the summertime for the town team. They were all older men. I was just a kid. I guess I was sixteen years old or something like that. And that's where I started. And then of course I went to college at Kansas State University and I pitched there for three years.

I ended up signing with the Detroit Tigers. Brooklyn offered me $500 a month, and Detroit, I signed with them for $450. And the reason I did was because the scout that scouted me knew me very well, and he said he thought I had a better chance getting into the major leagues with a young ball club than I did with Brooklyn, who had a bunch of older players.

When I was in the minor leagues, of course there were no lights. It was all day games and I was making $450 a month during the season. The top pay limit in the 3-I League in those days was $150 a month. So I'd get a check from the Decatur baseball team and then I'd get the rest of it from Detroit.

We traveled by bus all over Illinois, Indiana. The 3-I League was Indiana, Iowa, and Illinois. And we all traveled by bus and it was a hard life.

When I was a youngster I threw the conventional way over the top. But I played three years of college football at Kansas State University and prior to the first game we played, we played Purdue as the opening game, and just about a week before we played, I tackled and I got, what they called a knockdown shoulder, but I think what they call it today is a separation.

I couldn't get my arm up to throw and I was doing the kicking and I wasn't doing the passing. But I had that injured twice. And I got to the point where in baseball, I kept getting a little lower. And my last year in school I was throwing sidearm.

When I went to Decatur and they farmed me out, the manager down there was a guy name of Bob Coleman. Bob watched me throw and he said, "Elden, if you're going to pitch in the major leagues, you're going to have to get the ball over the plate!"

And he said, "So many of the sidearm pitchers have trouble with control." He said, "I'd like to see you get right down underneath and line up with the plate right from underneath. Just as low as you can get." So he says, "You're in line with it rather than being over the top." He said, "You'll be down here."

So I tried pitching batting practice for three or four days and it was pretty natural for me. And we were playing Quincy. They were leading in the league and they came in to play us on a Monday I guess it was, and he said, "Elden," he said, "You're going to pitch the game against Quincy."

He said, "You're going to pitch nine innings. I don't care how many men you walk or how many hits they get off of you." He said, "You're out there for nine innings and I don't want you to throw any other way except directly underhand." Well, I did, and I struck out 15 men and I walked 2 men. And I think they got three or four hits off of me. But I won the ball game and from that day on that's all I ever pitched.

I threw a sinkerball and the curveball and the screwball. I get over the top of it underneath and break low and break away. And my fastball and sinkerball. And the curveball, to a left-hand hitter broke up inside and broke away from a right-hander.

The first time I was ever in New York, Bucky Harris was our manager, in 1933, and the first time I ever saw Yankee Stadium, why Bucky put me down in the bullpen.

We had a pitcher name of Carl Fischer. He got in trouble the third inning and Bucky called me in. I made that long walk from left field in. And the first hitter I pitched to, the first one in Yankee Stadium, was Babe Ruth. I threw four pitches and struck him out. And then I got Lou Gehrig out. I think he lined to Greenberg at first.

So I go out to start the next inning, and they had a third base coach by the name of Artie Fletcher. And he was what they used to call a first class (bench) jockey. He was an old-timer. He was probably forty years old. I thought he was pretty old at that time. But anyway, I go out to warm up and he says, "Hey, Bush. Bush, look over here." Calling me busher, you know.

I didn't pay any attention and I was loosening up. Pretty soon he says, "You can hear me." He said, "You've got the Bam [Ruth, the Bambino] all upset." He said, "He came back to the bench and said he had been struck out a lot of times and that was the first time a damn woman ever struck him out!" And the reason I remember that is because that upset me. If I had gotten my hands on Fletcher, I'd have choked him to death. 'Cause he kind of upset me with that remark. Making fun of me! But later I played with Babe. I played golf with Babe for three years in the wintertime in Florida.

I saw Babe that winter and I said to him, I said, "Did you tell Fletcher that I pitch like a woman?"

He says, "No, I didn't."

So I told him the story.

He says, "Well that sounded like Fletcher." He said, "I never said that!" He was a great guy.

When I first reported to Detroit to Mr. (Frank) Navin, I went to the Detroit Leland Hotel. That's where I stayed. That's just two or three blocks from the ballpark. I don't think it's there anymore. But that was a conventional hotel, but they also had live-in apartments on the upper floor.

And there were five men—I'll never forget those fellows because they were five bachelors and they all lived there in the hotel and they saw every game the Tigers had ever played. And when I got there, the first night I was there, why, I had dinner with these fellows. They were really five great men. And, of course, they knew I was a rookie coming up and they wanted to know where I came from. It had been in the papers that I was coming in.

I was there about ten days, pitching batting practice before the Tigers went on a trip before I went to Decatur. And while we were there, they told me about the deal with (Leo) Durocher. They were there when it happened. Babe had been—first the Yankees had a problem getting someone to room with Babe, because he was always prowling around at night and eating midnight snacks and doing other things and didn't sleep much.

And here is at a time when a young fellow got off of a road trip he was exhausted, because he hadn't had too much sleep because of Babe. But when Durocher joined the ball club, he was Ruth's roommate and no problem. Everything was fine. But about the second or third trip they took, Babe thought he was spending more money than he usually did and he had lost a gold watch.

So the story goes, as they told me, that Babe planted some marked bills, supposedly $100 bills, five of them, and they turned up missing and his gold watch was gone. It was in Detroit when he found out that Durocher was asleep and he came in and he went in Durocher's bag and found the $500 and the gold watch in it.

Babe went over and got Durocher out of bed and they had to almost break the door down he was about to kill him. These guys said they had to get someone up there with a key and unlock it, because they were making so much noise. Durocher was gone the

Mickey Cochrane

next day. Never played with the Yankees again. Never played in the American League again.

In 1933 Bucky Harris was our manager. And that winter, why Mr. Navin spent $100,000 and bought Mickey Cochrane from the Philadelphia Athletics. And that was the first year that we trained in Lakeland, Florida. And so when we got down there we stood in awe to see Mickey Cochrane because he was the greatest catcher in baseball, and we were just a bunch of kids.

Schoolboy Rowe and the rest of us, Hank Greenberg, we were just youngsters. And after he was there about ten days or so, he said, "You know," he says, "we've got enough talent on this ball club to win the American League pennant." Well, we looked at each other and thought, well you know, he's got a lot of confidence in us. Well, he kept talking about this thing. And so, we had—we had some talent I guess if you want to call it that.

We had Hank Greenberg at first base, and Charlie Gehringer at second base, Billy Rogell at shortstop, Marvin Owen at third base, Goose Goslin in left field, and Jo-Jo White in center field, and then we had two other fielders, with Pete Fox and Gerald Walker [Greenberg, Goslin, Cochrane, and Gehringer are all Hall of Famers]. And they would interchange in various games.

We were just a bunch of young fellows that had hardly been in the league, you know. And they're talking about winning a pennant. Well, Mickey was one of the most inspirational leaders I've ever seen. He could carry a pitcher through the ball game. He told us pitchers, I'll never forget this, after we'd been there about ten days or so, Mickey said—he called the pitchers together and he said, "Look," he said. "I'm the catcher and I'm also the manager."

He said, "When you're pitching a ball game, you're on that mound," he said. "That ball game belongs to you." And he said, "I never want you to ever throw a pitch to me that you don't want to throw. If I call for a fastball and you want to throw the curveball, you just tell me and that's what we're going to throw." And he said, "If they hit it out of the ballpark, that's your fault. If we strike them out, that's my fault." So he said, "Just remember during the season never throw a pitch to me that you never want to—that you don't feel like you want to throw it."

Well, as a result of that, that certainly put all of us, I think, at ease. Because we didn't feel the pressure we had to do what he had to say. But after working with Mickey, game after game, you got to the point where your minds were working the same. Seldom you'd ever shake him off. If you did, you shook him off just for the hitter's benefit. But that's the way Mickey handled the pitching staff.

That's why if he had a bunch of young pitchers, that's the way he'd carry them through. We had a first baseman, Hank Greenberg, who's kind of an interesting story I think. Hank was six foot five and he weighed about 210, 212 pounds—long, gangly guy. And at first base, when he first came up, he's just about as awkward as you could get. He was flat-footed and he had trouble shifting his feet around.

He had another problem with a pop-up fly. Hank had trouble fielding that pop fly. Oh, we had a third base coach the name of Del Baker, and he used to hit what we call fungos, you know. Well, he'd get Del Baker out there in the morning before the ball game at 9:00 in the morning, and was hitting fly balls straight up in the air so Hank could catch 'em. Hank got so he could catch that ball in his hip pocket.

He made himself—he worked on his weaknesses constantly whether it was hitting or playing first base—shifting his feet at first. And he later became, to me, one of the greatest first basemen that ever played the game. One reason, he was so big. You know, he was six foot five and he had big long arms. And when he stretched out at first base he was almost behind the pitcher.

I mean, that's overexaggerating it a little, but I think he picked up probably a half a step against the runner with that long reach he had. And Charlie Gehringer was a guy that, I don't know, he was what they call the mechanical man. He just played second base like no one I've ever seen. Charlie was always in position it seemed when the hitter hit the ball to the right side of the field.

Charlie was either over here when he hit and the same guy came up to the bat and he'd hit it over here and Charlie would be over there. And he was a—I think his lifetime batting average was something like .321 or something like that. [It was .320.] One of the great, great second baseman. We had Billy Rogell, who was the shortstop. Billy was a switch-hitter and was very fast, had a very good arm, and an excellent fielder.

The two, the combination of Rogell and Gehringer, was the best, I think, best in baseball at that particular time. And Billy, incidentally, died about three weeks ago or so, at the age of ninety-eight. And Billy and I were the last two on that club that were alive, and I'm the only one left.

Marvin Owen was a college boy out of San Clara University. Great, great hands, great fielder, and was up around the .280, .290 mark sometimes. I think in 1935 he might have hit .300. [He hit .317 in 1934 and .263 in 1935.] At one time we had every—every fielder, outfielder, infielder, all hitting .300 at one time.

Mickey Cochrane had a great arm, very accurate. He was a great receiver. He was a kind of chunky guy, you know, and he sat back there and he had a great set of hands. And he was with you all the time; he just concentrated so hard on what was going on. And you got to the point where you just almost thought like he did, you know, he wanted you to—and concentration.

Mickey was also—he was a left-hand hitter. And I think he had a batting average of over .300, lifetime batting average [.320]. And he was—he was fast, very fast, and he was all over the field when the play was at first base—he was backing up first all the time, you know. But Mickey was one of the great, great catchers of the game at that particular time.

Hank Greenberg

We played the Cardinals in the '34 World Series. Frankie Frisch was the manager. They had Dizzy and Paul Dean and Durocher played shortstop. Pepper Martin was at third base. And I can't think of the players right at the time. But they had a great ball club.

I won my ball game. The first one I pitched was in St. Louis. I beat the Cardinals in I think the fourth game. And then I started against Dizzy Dean in the seventh game. And that was a game when Joe Medwick, he was an outfielder—left fielder—caused a big fuss.

He and Marvin Owen had a little to-do—Medwick slid into third base with his spikes high and caught Marvin's shirt with his spikes. And Marvin took the ball and started ramming it down his neck. And they started a little scuffle and of course they had scored, I think. I went into the third inning. Got the bases loaded and Frankie Frisch hit a ball off of Greenberg's glove. Greenberg jumped and touched it, and it went down against the wall in center field or right field.

They scored—ended up scoring seven runs in that inning. Well, by this time the fans were really upset. They were upset with a call that went against us at third base. And then when Medwick slid into third base, that really started something. When the inning was over Medwick went out in left field and the people started throwing everything that they'd brought out on the field.

A lot of them had been out there all night long because that was the seventh game and they had to buy tickets at the ticket office. And they had lined up there the night before and some of them stayed out there all night. They had their dinner with them and their breakfast, and all that garbage they'd brought with them. And they started throwing it from the stands at Medwick. It got to be kind of dangerous. They were throwing bottles and everything else. And finally, Judge Landis was there (Kenesaw Mountain Landis, the baseball commissioner). And Judge Landis called a halt and came out and walked out into the field and told Medwick to get out.

Took him out of the ball game. And that was, that inning I

think lasted something like three-quarters of an hour before they got things cleaned up. Because they had to go out and pick the junk off the left field. But anyway, Dizzy shut us out 11–0. We could hardly get a foul ball off of him. He was tough. He was a great pitcher.

I came back in '35 and won 18 games. I had my best year. I led the league in winning percentage.

We won the pennant early that year. And the Cubs won theirs— I pitched the opening game in Chicago. They opened up in Detroit with two games and then went to Chicago. And I pitched the third game and I left the ball game in the sixth or seventh inning. I pitched against Bill Lee. Bill Lee had led the National League in pitching that year, too.

So I left the ball game when it was 2-and-2, and we finally won the ball game in the 11th inning I believe it was, for that ball game. And then that series went six games. And Tommy Bridges pitched the sixth game. I was scheduled to pitch the seventh game of that— of that series. But, interesting thing, on the sixth game, Goose Goslin and I were sitting on the steps of the dugout watching the game, and we were at bat in the ninth inning.

And there were three hitters ahead of Goose and he said, "You know, I got a feeling I'm going to be out there with the winning run on base and we're going to win this ball game." And sure enough, that's what happened. Mickey Cochrane got on first base, I got on second base, and—and Goslin got his hit and won the ball game. And we came back. But I think it was the fifth game—fourth or fifth game—Hank Greenberg broke his wrist.

There was a throw at first base and I believe Phil Cavarretta, if I'm not mistaken, their first baseman, ran into him and the throw was over to the left of him, and he reached over to get it and Cavarretta run into him and broke his wrist. So he was out the last three games I believe. But we went ahead anyway and got by without him. We missed him! He was one of the strengths of our ball club.

•   •   •

You know they had some great hitters on the Yankees. Of course they always had them. Joe came up in '36, I believe it was. But they had an outfielder, the name of Tommy Henrich. And that guy gave me more trouble than anybody on the Yankee ball club. I had fairly good success with DiMaggio. He told me he had trouble picking up my ball.

But they had Bill Dickey who was the catcher. He's one of the great ones. I think he probably, in my opinion, was one of the great catchers ever in the American League. Of course they had Gehrig. Gehrig was a low-ball hitter. And, of course, my best pitch was a sinkerball. And I was pitting my strength against his strength, which was dangerous at times. But I found that if I kept the ball low and threw at his feet, he'd have to get his feet out of the way, because he'd walk into the hitter's box and he'd always take his left foot, kind of screw it into the ground.

He had legs about that big around. And he'd plant that leg, and he hit practically flat-footed. And so I found out if I could keep that left foot loose he couldn't get hold of it so good.

One time I fractured his toe. He didn't get his foot out of the way. He kept saying to me—we used to talk to each other underneath the dugout, and in the stands before the game. He says, "You know, damn you," he said, "you're throwing at my feet."

And I said, "What'd I throw at your feet for? If I was going to hit you, I'd hit you in the head where it wouldn't hurt ya." And we had a joke about it. But one day he didn't get his foot out of the way.

Bill McGowan was the umpire and it hit him, evidently, right square on the big toe on his left foot. And of course those shoes were made out of kangaroo skin and they were very, very thin. And he went down and Lou had a high voice, his voice was a little high. He's lying on the ground and holding his toe, and he said, "Bill, I told you he was throwing at my feet." He said, "Jesus, I think he broke my foot."

Bill said, "Aw, come on," he said. "Get up and go on down to first base, there's nothing wrong with you." Well, for the next several

Lou Gehrig and Babe Ruth

games he had an aluminum thing he put over the end of his toe. And he kept his [consecutive-games] streak going that way. But it almost, almost got him. But I didn't do it intentionally; he just didn't get his foot out of the way.

Babe was a big swinger. He'd turn his back; he'd turn his back to you like that. And when he missed, it pretty near took the air all out of the stadium. He'd take some real hard swings. And you could pull the string on him. And also keep it away from him. I either kept it away from him or pitched him on the inside and then changed up on him.

He got his hits, but I pitched against him in 1933, '34. And then he went over to the Boston Braves. But he was still dangerous. You

Joe Cronin

make a mistake and he could hurt you. They had a second baseman name of Tony Lazzeri, who was a great second baseman.

That Tommy Henrich, just stood there flat-footed and slapped the ball around. I could pitch him inside and he'd pull it. I could pitch it on the outside and he'd hit it to left field. But I got him out once in a while, but I had more trouble with him than any Yankee on the club.

They traded me to the Red Sox in 1939. And Joe Cronin was the manager. And we started off the season, we had two catchers, Johnny Peacock and Gene Desautels. And when we started the ball games, Cronin was on the mound as much as I was.

He'd run out there and grab the rosin bag and throw it down

and he'd say, "Make him hit the fastball; make him hit the curve-ball. You know, keep the ball down on him; keep it inside; keep it outside." And he just drove me crazy on the pitcher's mound. I couldn't concentrate. And I tried to shake the catcher off, and I was working a game and someone, Gene Desautels, the catcher, and he gave me two or three signs I didn't want to throw him.

I shook him off and finally I called him out there, and I said, "What the hell's the matter with you?" I said, "When I shake you off, I don't to want throw it."

And he said, "Well, don't talk to me," he said, "talk to Cronin. He's calling the pitches from shortstop."

Well, that—it was a psychological thing, I guess, for me. I prob-ably made a mistake by not going to Joe and saying, "Look, I've been in the league for six years, I've been pretty successful, and I would just like to pitch the ball game myself."

But I didn't do that. Lefty Grove, incidentally, when Cronin would start to the mound with Lefty Grove, Lefty Grove would go for the dugout. He wouldn't even talk to him. And so I had a bad year that year. I pitched the fewest innings and I just—I couldn't play for Joe. Joe was a nice person. He was a good ballplayer. But he was the most nervous guy at shortstop, and being a manager he tried to manage everything, you know.

We had a great ball club over there with Jimmie Foxx at first base, Bobby Doerr at second base, Joe Cronin at shortstop. We had Ted Williams up that year, Roger Cramer, Joe Vosmik.

That year we had a bad year, Mr. Yawkey called me in at the end of the season, and he said, "Elden," he said, "we'd like to have you sign a contract so we don't have to go to the mail."

I said, "Tom," I said, "you just signed Cronin to a five-year con-tract." And I said, "It's a waste of your money and my time because I cannot play for Joe Cronin."

I said, "He's a nice guy, but, he just drives me crazy on the pitcher's mound. I just can't—I can't play like that." So I said, "You either sell me, trade me, or else I'll retire." And so Fred Haney called me; he was the manager of the St. Louis Browns. Fred called me

Ted Williams

about, oh I guess, three weeks later. And he said, "I understand you're not going to sign with the Red Sox."

I said, "That's right."

He said, "Will you pitch for me?"

I said, "If you'll let me pitch the ball game, I will"

He said, "You can pitch the ball game if you come over here." Well, to make a long story short, in 1940, the Boston Red Sox finished I think eight games out of first place. The St. Louis Browns finished in sixth place and I won 16 ball games that year for Fred Haney. And I could have won more than that in Boston because they had a much better ball club. But it just seemed they never got the thing together.

•   •   •

Well Ted Williams was a—he had just turned twenty years of age. And I never saw a fellow that was more—had baseball on his mind twenty-four hours a day. We had a mirror in the clubhouse and you'd see Williams up there about every single day taking dry swings and studying his swing.

In spring training he would, he'd talk to everybody about, you know, how does Ruffing pitch, how does Gomez pitch, how does so-and-so pitch, and he'd just wear you out with questions. I think when we opened the season he knew about as much about the American League pitching as guys who'd been in the league for six years. But he was very studious and very bright. Ted was a very bright young man.

He didn't forget anything when you told him. And, so when the season started, I was rooming with Jimmie Foxx, he was my room-mate in Boston. And they both lived down at a hotel together. And Jimmie was in the midst of getting a divorce. His wife, Helen, she later married a banker on the Main Line in Philadelphia.

She was kind of a social climber and that was not good—Jim-mie had no interest in that. But, anyway, the two of them lived in a hotel and we used to—my wife, Mildred, and I—used to invite them out to the house. We had an apartment and we had them out there and Mildred made fried chicken for them. And Ted loved that fried chicken, so did Jim. So three or four times during the year, Jim was alone and Ted was alone, and so we had them out for fried chicken.

Ted to this very day, the day, well five days before he died, I guess, the last thing he says, he says, how's the queen. And I said she's great. He says give her my love. And that's about the last words that Ted Williams said to me over the telephone before he died about five or six days later.

Well, you know there's a lot of stories about Hank Greenberg being Jewish and about how the baseball players rode him and the fans got on him and everything. Well, I never saw that, I never saw that. Hank Greenberg, in Detroit, was worshipped by everybody, not just the Jews but the Protestants, the Catholics, and the colored and everybody else.

Hank Greenberg was such a great gentleman, a real true gentleman and there have been many stories written about this. One incident took place; we were playing the White Sox. Jimmy Dykes was the manager of the White Sox. And Jimmy Dykes was a good manager, but he was also one of the jockeys.

He was an agitator; it was his ball club against the other ballplayers. This particular day, Greenberg flied out or something and the visiting dugout was on the first base side and Greenberg was walking back to our dugout and we didn't pay any attention. It was just a regular out, you know.

When the game was over, Hank Greenberg's locker was in the corner. I was here and Tommy Bridges was the next one. We were next to Hank. Hank came in after the game and took off his outer shirt, put on his shower slippers, rubber slippers they had, and he walked out the door.

He was gone for just a few minutes and came back, I didn't pay attention, I thought he had a visitor or something, which we did lots of time. I didn't think anything about it. Well, the next day, [White Sox pitcher] Ted Lyons, I was talking to him in the runway, he said, "Jesus, boy was that Greenberg ever hot last night."

I said, "What do you mean?"

He said, "You know he came in our clubhouse?"

I said, "No. I didn't know."

He said, "He came in our clubhouse." He said, "He opened up the door and walked in and he stood there and he said, 'I want that guy that called me a yellow Jew SOB, I want him to stand up.' And Hank stood there, and he went all the way around the room, walked around. Not one guy moved a muscle and no one said one single word."

Hank came out and came in our room, went ahead and got in the shower; no one had ever said anything about it. But I'll tell you, the guy that said that was the luckiest guy in the world, because that Greenberg would have killed him. That was the only real time that I ever heard that anyone said anything, and I never heard anything derogatory about Hank Greenberg being a Jew, never. And I played with him for six years.

We were in Boston. I was working a game, I think against Lefty Grove. I was with first the Browns. And I had Grove beat 2-to-1 going into the ninth inning. This was the first year that Johnny Pesky came up. And Johnny Pesky hit just ahead of Ted (Williams).

So Pesky came to bat and he dumped a ball down to third base; Harlan Clift was our third baseman, and I was flat-footed on the mound; he beat it out. And so Ted was the next hitter; Bobby Swift was my catcher. And Bobby came out to me and said, "What do you think he's going to be doing? Trying to get him over, going to hit, or what'll he be doing?"

I said, "With Cronin mad he may have him bunting." I said, "I'll keep the ball outside. I'll keep it down; we'll see what he's going to do, whether he's going to square around just trying to hit it or whether he's really going to swing." Well, I threw the ball probably knee-high, and it was outside about so far [indicated approximately one foot] on the first pitch. Ted Williams reached out and he hit that ball in the center field bleachers just like a 2-iron—just "bang." And he got in that crazy lope, laughing all the way around.

Of course, the ball game's over. They win the ball game 3-to-2. And he was in the runway waiting for me when I came off the field. He was standing and waiting, laughing and joking, and I said, "Get away from me." I said, "I'm going to knock your head off."

He said, "I know what you told Swift." He said, "Let's just keep the ball outside and down and we'll find out what he's going to do." He said, "You threw that ball exactly where I knew you were going to throw it." And that was Ted Williams.

He was thinking every time he went to bat; he knew what he was doing up there and he knew that pitcher and he studied that pitcher. We'd be on the bench when we were playing a game and the guys would be talking about different things, watching different things. Pretty soon Williams would say, "You know, he started the last five hitters off with a curveball." We didn't even pay attention to him. But he had that guy; he had his eye on that pitcher all the time.

Jimmie Foxx

•   •   •

When I roomed with Jimmie Foxx in 1939, he was not a drinking man. I did not drink and when we were on the road we just would have a beer. Jimmie Foxx, we used to call him "The Beast," because he was so strong, so powerful, and he was such a pure hitter at the plate.

Yeah, he was about five-ten or -eleven, but, boy, he had muscles in his ears, we used to say. He could hit that ball so hard and made a lot of noise when he hit them. I'll tell you one instance I will never forget; we were in St. Louis playing the Browns and Jim had a sinus problem and in the summertime it really gave him a lot of trouble; he took drops and things for his nose.

One night we were in St. Louis and I was awake, I woke up, and Jim was in the bathroom and he had a nosebleed. His nose was bleeding like, I thought he was going to bleed to death. Well, I called the trainer and he came up and they packed him with ice and everything and they just kept going. That went on for at least two hours, maybe more, and he lost, I don't know how much blood, but he lost a lot of blood with a nosebleed.

They finally got it stopped and the next morning, I don't think he slept probably two hours during the night. The next morning I woke up and I said, "Jim," I said, "why don't you stay here and if you want something to eat for breakfast, I'll bring it up to you or you can order room service." I said, "You just stay here and sleep."

I went down for breakfast and I came back and he was still in bed; he didn't want anything to eat, so I went out to the ballpark about 10:30; I guess it was or 11:00 and he was still in bed. And I said, "Why don't you just stay in bed today?" I said, "Don't leave. We're playing the Browns so what difference does it make?"

Well, he said, "I'll think it over. You go ahead." So, I went on out and, just before the game started, Jimmie came out of the dugout all suited up and ready to go. The first time at bat, he hit a line drive in the center field stands in St. Louis that was about 428 feet, I think it was, to the center field bleachers. Well, he hit a ball just like a frozen rope into those stands in center field.

I'm telling you I was never so surprised; I absolutely couldn't believe a man could lose that much blood and have a night like he had and get up there and hit that ball like he did. He was a wonderful, wonderful hitter, great fielder. Had a good arm. He used to be a catcher at one time. He had an excellent arm and one of the nicest guys. Low-key, quiet person, always had a grin on his face, the nicest person in the world.

Lefty Grove was one of the greatest left-handed pitchers I ever saw. Boy, he could buzz that thing in there like crazy. He'd knock his mother down if she got too much of a hit off of him. He'd knock you flat on your back as soon as look at you, he was mean on that mound. He didn't like to lose. When you beat Lefty Grove, you really had to beat him.

He had great control. An interesting thing, he was in the minor leagues for about four or five years before he came to the major leagues. He threw every single day. He'd pitch a ball game today and the next day he'd go out and he'd pitch batting practice the next day. His theory was that you had to keep that arm strong, keep your legs strong and your arms strong. Lefty Grove never had a sore arm in his life.

Funny thing everybody asks me about baseball, and I was only in that about ten years, but I was in the abrasive business about thirty some years and no one ever asks me anything about abrasives.

One of my teammates in 1939 was Moe Berg. Well, Moe Berg was one of the most mysterious men I've ever known, and incidentally one of the smartest. He was a graduate of Princeton. But he was so secretive and he was so different. We'd go on a road trip and

Moe Berg

he had a little suitcase, wicker, wicker suitcase about that big, and I think he had probably two clean shirts in there and a couple pairs of socks and underwear.

The rest of it was newspapers. And he wore a black suit, year 'round, white shirt and black necktie. And that was the only clothes I ever saw Moe Berg ever wear.

Well, he went to Japan with that group that used to go over there in postseason and play against the Japanese. And Moe went along, he was on the club. And when the club got through playing—Moe spoke Japanese, fluent Japanese. And the Japanese people were crazy about him, because he can talk their language. Well, when the club came home Moe Berg stayed there.

He traveled all over Japan. And he could go anyplace. Well, it ended up he was over there for a reason. He brought back pictures and photos and everything of their war complex and he took pictures of everything. And he was, at that time, he was actually spying for the United States and nobody had any idea about that at all.

We'd never see him at the hotel. Only see him at the ballpark. And then after that we didn't know whether he had a girlfriend or what it was. But we kind of had a suspicion something was going on, but we didn't know. Nineteen thirty-nine there was a lot of things going on that we didn't know.

But he was with the government I'm sure at that particular time, doing work for them.

I had a call from some fan a couple of years ago, talking baseball, and he said, "Did you know that you have a home run batting record that's never been broken; you are a coholder of the home run record?"

I said, "No. I certainly did not."

He said, "You are one of six in the American League pitchers who hit two home runs in one game." He said, "That's been tied six times but," he says, "it's never been broken."

I didn't know that; I don't know whether it's been broken yet or not. Of course, in the American League, the pitchers don't hit anymore.

I think it was the Yankees' first trip (to Boston) in, in 1939. In Fenway Park they had a common runway between the clubhouses— when you come out of the clubhouse. The home team was on this side of the runway and the visitors on the other side. But we used the same runway coming out onto the field.

I'd been in the outfield, running, getting in my run. I'm going in to change my sweatshirt for the game. I wasn't pitching. I think Grove was working the game. And when I came out, Gehrig was standing in the runway with one foot up on the step of the dugout, and he's smoking a cigarette.

So I come walking down the runway—and I just went over and wrapped my arm around his neck. Well usually he'd lift you right off the ground. But I put my arm around his neck and he went down. He said, "Oh my God, don't do that."

Well, he just folded up. I had to help him up. And I said, "What's the matter with you?"

He said, "I don't know." He says, "I can't hit the ball out of the infield." He says, "I've just lost all my strength." He said, "I've had a terrible winter."

I said, "Well, when did you first notice it?"

And he said, "Well, it was right at the tail end of the season last year." But he said, "I've got something wrong with me. I don't know what it is."

Well, anyway, make a long story short, that was on Tuesday. And they played Wednesday and Thursday and then went to Detroit. And in the paper the next day on Friday, I believe it was, or Saturday, I read where he had gone to Mayo Brothers and they found that he'd had this disease. It was a sad deal.

Well, he had such a flat swing, Gehrig and Charlie Gehringer, both of them, very flat swings. And when they hit that ball, Charlie Gehringer hit more line drives that were caught. I'd say that 50 percent of the balls that were caught were line drives that he hit that could have been base hits, but they'd be right at somebody, whether right field or left field. Gehrig was the same way. You get that ball down there.

If you get up on Gehrig—Schoolboy Rowe and Tommy Bridges and those guys always tried to keep the ball up. Anything down below, they make a mistake and get down low and he could really crunch it. And he had so much power, powerful. We had that short right field. He could hit in there on a line drive before you could turn your head, practically.

But Babe was a different kind of hitter. DiMaggio was—he never took any stride either. But he stood flat-footed. But he had more fly balls. You could—you could get Joe to get that ball in the air so he didn't get it too far. But he had a lot of power, too.

Joe DiMaggio, I don't think he ever threw to the wrong base in his life. He'd get that ball and he knew exactly what he was going to do with it. And he took big long strides in running. He just glided. You know, he didn't run up and down, he just took big, long strides and just kind of glided into it. And he covered a lot of territory. And he was like Ted Williams also, in studying the hitters.

I don't think—[manager Joe] McCarthy I don't think ever moved Joe DiMaggio into any particular spot, you know, waving him over or waving him back or telling him anything like that. He just did it himself. Joe was a student of the game, as was Ted Williams. But Joe was such a compact hitter. He was strong and powerful and he could hit anything. He might hurt you anytime.

Lefty Grove was probably the greatest left-hander that I saw. Let's put Bobby Feller as one of the best right-handers. There were many good pitchers in those days. Red Ruffing for the New York Yankees, Lefty Gomez, Ted Lyons of the White Sox was a great pitcher.

Bobby Feller, when he first came up, boy he was wild. He would throw one over the top of your head and one behind your head and then one down the middle.

Incidentally, Bobby and I—when I was in St. Louis, we played

Cleveland, and pitched the first night game that ever played in St. Louis; I think it was in 1940. We each struck out 12 men. He struck me out four times. I struck him out three times, and he hit his first home run in the major leagues to beat me 3-to-2. I see him every once in a while. It was in St. Louis, and they have a short right field fence. And the ball went up and dropped in for a home run. The last time I heard him tell that, it was a line drive over the right field fence; its gets longer every year.

My last year in college I played in Manhattan, Kansas, and we had six of us in college; then we had some other players, semipro players, and they had a group called the Manhattan Travelers. We played about 30 or some games over Oklahoma, Kansas, Nebraska, around, barnstorming.

We played the Kansas City Monarchs twice. I pitched a game against Satchel Paige in Manhattan (Kansas) and we beat him 1-to-nothing. Later on, I pitched for a semipro team up in Nebraska, at the Arapaho County Fair. And the Monarchs played up there, and we played them.

They had a left-hander by the name of Oliver. I'll never forget him, I thought he was a better pitcher than Paige was. But, of course, they had so many of those guys—the Monarchs in those days, they were kind of a fun team. They played around if they'd get ahead of you. They didn't lose too many ball games because they had a great ball club. But when they saw they were into a ball game, they settled down and got pretty serious.

But I beat Paige 1-to-nothing and then I beat Oliver 2-to-1, up in Nebraska. But I never did see Paige pitch in the American League. Paige earned his publicity, the big deal, in what we called the *Denver Post* Tournament. The *Denver Post*, a paper out in Denver, used to hold a tournament every year for semipro teams. And in those days, the Kansas City Monarchs were not considered a professional team.

It was not recognized as a professional team, and they played in the *Denver Post* Tournament and they won it. Paige pitched five ball games in three days. He pitched and won all five ball games. He pitched four complete games, I think, or something like that in a five-day period. But he was, no doubt, a great pitcher, but how he was in the major leagues, I don't know.

The greatest players I saw? Mickey Cochrane was, I think, probably the greatest catcher I saw and I would rate Bill Dickey and Rick Farrell; Rick Farrell was a great receiver. He wasn't any power at the plate, little single hitter, sharp hitter, but was a great receiver.

Foxx was a muscle man and Greenberg had so much power, he took that big stride and had a big swing. Second base, I'd put Charlie Gehringer as number one and then they had Bobby Doerr for Boston, was a great second baseman, over there when I played, that was his first year up.

Tony Lazzeri, and then the other boy came in, followed Lazzeri, at second base, Joe Gordon. Joe was a good second baseman. And as shortstop, of course, you had Cronin. Cronin was a great ballplayer, no doubt about it, a great fielder. Frank Crosetti, he was a great shortstop who didn't get too much publicity, but he was an excellent shortstop. In the outfield you had so many of them, I guess. Goose Goslin, Ted Williams, Joe DiMaggio.

Well, I think probably I would like to say this, I think of all the experiences that I had in the ten years of major leagues, I met so many great people, great players in the Hall of Fame. And, of course, I am not in the Hall of Fame, but I knew these fellows, I played with them and I knew them personally.

And I think that what I would say that I don't know how I'll be remembered, but I just want to say this, that I feel that I have probably been one of the luckiest guys that ever played because coming from a little town out in western Kansas, 400 people population, and then have the privilege of playing Major League Baseball for ten years and knowing all of these men personally.

I can just say that I am very grateful for baseball, I think I played in the period of baseball when it was a wonderful period. We didn't have the problem with dope or alcohol or steroids or anything like that. We were just a bunch of young men trying to make a living and doing something that we all liked to do and to make a living, get paid to play a game; I think you have to be very fortunate; I was very fortunate and I will always be grateful to everybody for that opportunity.

BOB FELLER

Bob Feller's mound accomplishments are legendary—including fanning 17 batters in one game at the age of seventeen, tossing 3 no-hitters and 12 one-hitters, and leading the league in strikeouts seven times despite losing almost four years in his prime due to military service. But Washington Senators manager Bucky Harris may have summed up the fireballing right-hander best when he told his players, "Go on up there and hit what you see. If you can't see it, come on back."

Feller began pitching with the Cleveland Indians in 1936 before he had even finished high school. After several relief appearances, Feller made his first start on August 23 and fanned 15 St. Louis Browns in a 4–1 victory. Famed for the speed of his fastball, and arguably one of the hardest throwers of all time, Feller also had a devastating, if overlooked, curveball.

"Rapid Robert" would soon become the game's top pitcher, averaging 25 wins a season and leading the league in strikeouts from 1939–41. But after Japan bombed Pearl Harbor he enlisted in the Navy and would miss most of the next four seasons. Feller would return to the game full-time in 1946, winning 26 games, and would remain a Cleveland fixture for the next ten years.

After ending his 18-year big league career with 266 victories and 2,581 strikeouts, Feller was elected to the National Baseball Hall of Fame in 1962.

I'M FROM VAN METER, IOWA, which is a town right down on Interstate 80, where I have a museum. It's eighteen miles west of Des Moines on Interstate 80 along the Raccoon River. When I was going to school there, riding the bus, our farm was three miles northeast of Van Meter.

One of my classmates said to me one time when I was a kid in the second grade, or maybe even the first grade—probably the second grade—"Let's go over to the ball diamond." I didn't know what the word "ball diamond" meant, but he did. And all of a sudden, I realized this. We walked over to the ball diamond. And shortly

Bob Feller

thereafter, I started playing catch with my dad, throwing the ball when I was a kid. Even before that, he'd roll a ball from the living room into the kitchen and I'd pick the ball up; I couldn't catch it yet. It was a rubber ball. And I'd throw it through the door. Once in a while, I'd miss the door and knock a little plaster off the wall. He would catch me, sitting on the davenport with a pillow. And sooner or later, why then, we got the real baseball and started playing catch in the yard. He bought me my glove at the Hopkins Sporting Goods store, in Des Moines. And it was a Rogers Hornsby glove. Rogers Hornsby, of course, was a hero of mine and I did pitch against him later on when he was managing and coaching third base for the St. Louis Browns. In 1936 and '37, he'd pinch-hit. That was way, way, way before the DH.

And then, we took some two-by-fours and built a little batting cage over in the pasture. My dad would pitch batting practice to me. And I had a dog by the name of Tagalong. Tagalong was our outfielder—Tagalong and my sister, who was nine years younger than I.

I had a post on a couple of two-by-fours—we put it in the batter's box on the left side and the right side. He'd move it forward and backward and all over the batter's box. So it was—tried to simulate the batter with a different strike zone—the tall guy, the short guy. And I'd hold men on base. I did the whole thing.

When I was a little kid, I used to try taking my windup, the short pump handle and the big pump handle, a lot of motion, and coordination. And I'd always practice in the living room, in the winter, or in the barn, and, not throwing, just do simulations. And, so I could get my body behind the pitch, from the ball of your right foot to the tip of your fingers, get up and down your right side.

And we'd play in the pasture, and eventually, we built a ball diamond there. So that was the beginning. When I was nine, I went down with my dad to get a ball from Babe Ruth when the Larrupin' Lous and Bustin' Babes were playing in Des Moines at the Des Moines Demons' ballpark. It was the Des Moines Demons in those days, in the Western League. So they were selling baseballs for $5 autographed by Lou Gehrig and Babe Ruth.

We had our own team—loaned the uniforms to the high school in Van Meter. And, of course, I also played basketball in Van Meter, and we had our own team there. And I played four years of American Legion baseball at Des Moines, Iowa.

I started out playing second base; I played third base; I played shortstop. Well, I always pitched a little. And I could throw; I had a very good arm ever since I was a little kid about nine. And everybody would stand around and watch and when I threw a ball, I could throw it much further than any kid anywhere near my age.

I started pitching regularly when I was fifteen, when I was playing for an American Legion team in Des Moines. And I was the first American Legion graduate to be inducted into the Hall of Fame. And Ted Williams is the second one. Ted played American Legion ball in San Diego. And every year, I give the American Legion Outstanding Player in the United States, present him with a four-year college scholarship, which is sponsored by the American Legion from Indianapolis. We do this at the Hall of Fame, prior to the Hall of Fame game, which is always on a Monday. And we choose—they choose the player of the year and American Legion has a great program.

And then I had the heroes like Eddie Rickenbacker [the World War I ace pilot] and Rogers Hornsby and Babe Ruth. And I knew Walter Johnson well. And they were all heroes of mine.

We'd play in the barn and my dad was catching me one time and he squatted down—it was getting dusk. And he—I was going I was practicing curveballs. And so he gave me two fingers. He wanted me to throw a curveball. It was so dark, I only saw one finger; I thought it was a fastball. I was about fifteen years old, maybe fourteen, and I threw it as hard as I could.

We were about the end of our session. And I threw the pitch and hit him right above the heart and broke three ribs. And that put my—that was the reason for my picture being on the front page of *Time* magazine back in 1937. It was on the front of *Time* that I broke my dad's ribs. That was about the last time he caught me. I was getting to throw pretty hard.

There was a pitcher from Des Moines. I do not recall his name.

And he told me when I was a kid—very young—he said, "You sit over on the end of a piano bench or a chair and put the heels of your hand on the bench and let your rear end go down to the floor; extend your legs and push yourself up with your triceps." He said, "It's more important to have good triceps than to have good biceps."

So every day, I'd do twenty to thirty of these push-ups. And I'd get up and I'd do deep knee bends and take deep breaths. So because I had a tendency to kind of roll my shoulders over, I've always done that to develop my triceps for your extender muscles. And I also hit the speed bag a lot, and the punching bag that my dad bought me with a pair of mitts to help my extender muscles.

Whether it had any effect on my pitching, I don't know. I think it did. And I always recommend this to kids—on your fingertips and doing all this. I did a lot of physical exercise besides the work on the farm—driving the horses and then plowed ground and pitching bundles and cleaning the barns out on Saturday. And I did a lot of manual labor, and I think that's one thing that the kids don't do now. Long before you're even a teenager—when you're nine, ten, twelve years old—doing all this before you get into the gymnasium and use all this fancy, heavy-chromed equipment.

I never had any idea of doing anything but being a major league ballplayer from day one. Now, I'm sure there are a lot of young boys that—just like Tiger Woods: That's all he ever was going to be. This was all I was ever going to be. I never had any idea I wouldn't be successful. Now, this was pretty cocky for a little kid. And I worked at it—no candy.

My father and mother had strict values. Take care of yourself, listen, work hard, and try to profit by your mistakes. And, to be self-sufficient, depending on yourself. Tell the truth, be honest, and hopefully that you're successful.

My father never told me that he thought I'd be a professional ballplayer. But when I was fifteen we did take in the 1934 World Series in St. Louis and saw Dizzy and Paul Dean. I got to know them later and pitch against the Cardinals in an exhibition game in

Cleveland in 1936. And we saw the Tigers and the Cardinals in St. Louis, in Sportsman's Park. In fact, I pitched the first night game ever played in St. Louis in the major leagues in Sportsman's Park in 1940. And so I said to my dad, I said, "Those fellows look pretty good, but I think I can make it," on driving home.

In American Legion baseball, umpires were what you call bird dog scouts—so are high school coaches and traveling salesmen. The queen bee scout from the area—and there's always a queen bee scout in every area—well, the queen bee scout for the Cleveland ball team was Cy Slapnicka from Cedar Rapids. And he'd been told by the umpires. John McMahon was an umpire. And he told Cy Slapnicka that I had a good arm.

So Cy Slapnicka came down the following spring to buy Claude Passeau from the Des Moines ball club for the Cleveland club. Claude Passeau later came to the big leagues and I pitched against him in the All-Star Games and started an All-Star Game against him in 1946 in Fenway Park when Ted hit the blooper pitch for a home run. To go back to 1935: Cy Slapnicka had come down to buy Claude Passeau, to see him pitch on a Sunday. And I was pitching in an amateur game.

So he wanted to come over to see me and take a look and probably tell the scout that I was not a prospect. So he came to this ball game and he sat on the bumper right behind home plate and he saw me pitch. And he sat there and sat there and sat there. And this is a story he tells me; I didn't even notice him. And he never left. He never went to see Claude Passeau at the Des Moines ballpark that Sunday afternoon. He did come and approach my dad and my mother and me and we talked.

And he came back about ten days later—and I signed up. I was sixteen.

I pitched sandlot ball here in Cleveland and the St. Louis Cardinals came to town for an exhibition game. And I was going to go to Fargo in a couple days, and they wanted to save their pitching staff for this exhibition game. The money went to pay for the medical bills for the 20,000 sandlotters playing baseball in the city of Cleveland at the time on the sandlots, of all ages.

So they asked me if I'd like to pitch the fourth, fifth, and sixth innings in this exhibition game against the Cardinals. And I said I would love to, or something to that effect. I said, "Okay." So I go to the ballpark and pitch the fourth, fifth, and sixth inning against the Gashouse Gang. Leo Durocher was my first hitter, also my first strikeout. Frankie Frisch was going to be the second hitter, the manager. He saw me pitch a little while—I threw a couple balls behind Durocher, one over his head. And I got two strikes over (on Durocher) and he went to the dugout. The umpire said, "Get back here. You have another strike coming."

And he said, "You take it from me. I'm going to get a drink of water."

And Frisch took himself out of the lineup. He said, "There's no way I'm going to go up against that kid." And he put in a pinch hitter. And Frankie Frisch never came to bat. And that was my first—instead of going to Fargo the next day, they gave me a ticket to Philadelphia, where I joined the Cleveland Indians.

I got off at the 30th Street Station and went over to the ballpark, got dressed in the clubhouse, and shook hands with all the guys—my teammates and (manager) Steve O'Neill—and walked out there in the dugout. I was the first one there. And I looked up and here comes Connie Mack [the longtime Philadelphia Athletics manager] across from the Athletics dugout. And I knew I was the only fellow in the dugout; I knew he was going to see me. So I get up and I walk over behind the batting cage and they're taking batting practice. He said, "Welcome to the American League, Mr. Feller." I hadn't the slightest idea how he knew me. And probably he had read a few things in the paper that morning or a couple days before. And I loved Connie Mack; he was a dear friend of mine—a dear friend.

I was in the big leagues at seventeen. I'm the youngest pitcher to ever win a game in the major leagues. I'm also the youngest pitcher to ever lose a game in the major leagues.

After my game against the Cardinals, I pitched games, mopped up games that were lost; I went in to pitch five or six times before I got my first start, against the St. Louis Browns. I won that ball game, struck out 15, and, won it, I think, 4-to-1.

And then, I wound up winning five and losing three. Later, I struck out 17 Athletics at the age of seventeen, in September. And then I went to pitch in Fargo, that fall, in an exhibition game, in the new ballpark.

I believe the salary was $175 a month. I know, it was pretty good pay. I don't think anybody except Babe Ruth was making a whole lot more than that. Maybe, of course, Babe was, back, what-ever year it was he got the $80,000 contract from Jacob Ruppert, the big beer baron who owned the Yankees.

And, then my next year, I signed a contract for, what is an unreal amount, of $15,000, which is probably about the top salary of any Cleveland ballplayer, I don't know. But, my father had brain cancer, starting in the fall of 1936, I think, at the Mayo Clinic. And it was inoperable; they had to use X ray and radium. And that spring, be-fore we went to spring training in New Orleans, the Cleveland ball club paid all his hospital bills. It was over $10,000. I got to know Lou Gehrig's doctor up there, Dr. O'Leary, about three years before Lou Gehrig ever met him. I knew all the doctors that headed the de-partments, and also Dr. Will Mayo, from the Mayo Clinic.

I was never nervous when I was on the mound. I always figured that I had done as much work as I could, and I was as well prepared for the game as my adversary, who would be the batter, of course. And, Lyn Lary was my first, the leadoff man in my first big league game, against the Browns. I struck him out to start the game, and struck him out to finish the game.

I was a two-pitch pitcher until 1940, when I started throwing sliders. I did throw a changeup on my curveball, so I might be a two-and-a-half-pitch pitcher. But I never threw a changeup on my fastball, because I wasn't much good. I could throw an easy; it's easy to throw a curveball changeup, by just spinning it and cutting back a little. And then when I got the slider, it made it much better, particularly against left-hand hitters. I tried to keep it inside, partic-

Rogers Hornsby

ularly against the good hitters like Ted Williams, who was the great-est hitter I ever pitched to.

And, of course, followed, the next best hitter to him, if not just as good, was Rogers Hornsby, who I pitched against four or five times, when he was managing and coaching third base and also pinch-hitting for the St. Louis Browns. He played a couple games in 1936, at second base, which was his position. He also played 20 games in 1937. And he was a very tough hitter, stood way back in the box. He was our batting coach in 1947.

I learned by the trial-and-error method. We had, we'd have clubhouse meetings, and talk about the hitters. When I first came up, they wouldn't even let me come to the meeting to talk about the hitters' strengths and weaknesses.

They just told me to go out there and start throwing. And, after a couple of years, we did talk about, when my control got better. I became a pretty good pitcher in 1939. Up until then, I was a thrower. I had my best All-Star appearance in Yankee Stadium in 1939, when I came in with the bases full, and the American League was leading 3-to-1, and, with one out. And I threw a double-play ball to Arky Vaughan on the first pitch, and got out of the inning in the sixth inning. I relieved Tommy Bridges, a great pitcher for the Tigers, a great pitcher, good friend of mine.

And, then pitched the seventh, eighth, and ninth and allowed one hit. And that was my first and best appearance in the All-Star Game, even though I didn't receive the win, I got a save. There wasn't any such thing [as a save] in those days. I did get the win in 1946 in Fenway Park.

I had three days of rest, and once in a while I'd pitch with two days of rest, but rarely. And, sometimes you'd come in and relieve an inning or two, a hitter or two generally speaking. In 1946, my first year out of the Navy, I pitched 36 complete games, on three days' rest. We didn't have a great ball club that year. We finished, I think, sixth in an eight-club league. And, the manager was Lou Boudreau, who was a great manager, and a great ballplayer and a Hall of Famer, and my dear friend.

I pitched 36 complete games, which is the most complete games, from today till 1916, when Walter Johnson and Grover Cleveland Alexander pitched 36 and 38 complete games. It was the old dead ball, which went out in 1920.

I said to Cy Slapnicka, with whom I was having dinner on December 7, 1941, "I'm going to join the Navy."

He said, "Well, that's your choice."

I hadn't even told my parents yet. And I did. Gene Tunney, the world championship fighter, was the head of the Navy physical fitness program. He flew out to Chicago, and signed me up, in the Navy, three days after Pearl Harbor, at 8:00 in the morning on the 10th of the month. I went to War College after boot camp in Norfolk. After War College, I formed a baseball team in Newport, Rhode Island, for the Navy. And got the uniforms, got a schedule for them, went back to Norfolk for another gunnery course, before going on the *Alabama.* I played a couple games there. We played the Seabees. The Seabees started there, at Little Creek, right near Ocean View, Virginia, right near Norfolk.

Aboard the battleship *Alabama,* I was on the guns. I was a gun captain. I was a chief petty officer. And we went to take supplies to Russia. Then we went back and took MacArthur out of the Philippines.

Well, I'm no hero. The heroes never returned. The survivors returned. And that's the way I sincerely feel about it. I'm not saying this for a cliché. And, sure, there were some that didn't come. I remember the first hero we had was Colin Kelly. And he got killed; he was flying a dive-bomber. And he dove into a stack of a Japanese warship, and blew it up and sank it.

I remember, when they had the Army-Navy World Series in Honolulu. I was with the Third Fleet, way out in the Pacific, between the Marianas and the Philippines, and the captain came to me, and he said, "Bob, they want you to come back, and participate in the Army-Navy baseball World Series in Honolulu."

And I said, "Captain," I said, "I'm staying with you."

He said, "I knew before I asked you, that you'd stay here. I knew you wouldn't go."

I said, "Well, thank you."

So, he radioed them back, Feller's staying on the *Alabama.* And I think it was the right decision.

The *Alabama* was the only warship in the Third Fleet that didn't lose anyone to enemy action; we lost about thirty-six men to accidents aboard ship, which did happen, particularly during night firing.

Well, I got out the 23rd or 24th of August 1945 and came back and started pitching for the Indians. I pitched at Great Lakes [Naval Station]; I got myself in condition when I got back here.

My first game back here, in Cleveland in '45, they had the

mayor and the governor. The headline of the Cleveland morning paper said: "This is what we've all been waiting for." I pitched against Detroit and Hal Newhouser that night, night game we had; we didn't quite fill all the stadium, we had between 50,000 and 60,000, welcome me home, which was a great tribute. By the time the game was over, I was so tired I could have slept for a month. We won the ball game; I struck out 12.

In '45 I won five, lost three. In fact when I started the game in Yankee Stadium against Spud Chandler, he was still in the Army. We won it 10-to-3, and I met Spud that night in the hotel. He said, "I'm in terrible shape, I'm still in the Army. I shouldn't even be here." He was in uniform; I was not. I was out of uniform. I came back next spring training, early the next year, had a baseball school, sponsored by sporting goods companies.

Commissioner Happy Chandler told me, he said, "If you want to have a baseball school for a rehab program for the men in the military, I will give you thirty days of spring training instead of ten." So I got hold of the city of Tampa; we had 186 players there, had six ball diamonds, and the sporting goods companies furnished the equipment for players that had played major league ball or minor league ball or outstanding college players.

The newspapers helped greatly. Taylor Spink of the *Sporting News* helped to promote it, and Connie Mack was there every day with Al Lang, who was the first man to get the major league teams to go to Florida spring training. And Connie got there every day; he signed up a lot of players, starting farm systems again, and they gave bonuses to a few of them. And that was in January. We trained in Clearwater, so I stayed there and started my spring training really in January. I had all major league instructors and it cost me about $2,500, of my own money, and we were there for a month.

Of course I pitched against Satchel Paige in the Black All-Stars before the war. After the war we formed the barnstorming tours. Of course, it was segregated. I knew all the good ballplayers from the Monarchs and the Crawfords and the Newark Eagles, where Monte Irvin played, and I knew who could play and who couldn't play.

They don't need to tell me about who was the best Afro-American ballplayers.

Oh yes, we had Afro-American—of course, everyone called them black in those days—hired men on our farm. And they did a very good job. They'd come out there wanting to work, give them $30 a month and board and room and bonuses. My dad used to give anybody who didn't smoke, he'd give them an extra $5, but don't ever smoke around our farm buildings. If you did, you're going down the road the next day.

You couldn't play Negro League teams below the Mason-Dixon line. I mean, you could play in Cincinnati. We did. You couldn't play in Louisville; you couldn't even play in Phoenix. You wouldn't even think about playing in Atlanta, or any of the states below the Mason-Dixon line. New Orleans, no. But we did do very well; we played in Comiskey Park and Cleveland, New York, St. Louis, Kansas City.

I think your ability should get you the job, period. And if you can't do it with your ability, go learn how to do this. I know it's difficult, and if somebody was asking me a question which was on air the other day, what would you do if you were black? I say, "I don't know, probably the same thing I do if I were white, go to work." But I do know there's prejudice and I've heard it. I don't believe in the bigots, I never have. Neither had my father or mother, or any of our family.

We discussed barnstorming with a Negro League team just before World War II broke out, and I discussed it with other people. But when I was aboard ship I thought about this a lot. So as soon as I came out, and started my year in 1946, I got hold of the Wilkinson family, Mr. J. L. Wilkinson. He owned the Monarchs; he was in Des Moines, Iowa. They were the big team of course. I thought about it, got hold of Wilkinson; we made a deal. I ran the whole thing. I had a man out ahead ten days, Bob Hope's brother, Jack Hope. We sold scorecards with the beautiful program with all the blacks in it, and the whites.

I had Stan Musial on the team and Mickey Vernon, and Charlie Keller and Vince DiMaggio, Bob Lemon; I can go on and on and on, who I had on my team. I have the program, I still have some programs, and they have reproduced that program, which is being sold in my museum. We had a great trip. We drew over 400,000 people. In fact, we played in Yankee Stadium on a Friday night, early in October and Sunday afternoon that was the year [1946] that the Cardinals beat the Red Sox in seven games in the World Series, when Enos Slaughter scored from first on a single.

We played in Newark; Monte Irvin played against us, and the Newark Eagles. We played in Cincinnati; we played across the United States, Des Moines, Omaha; and we played up and down the West Coast, all the way from Vancouver to San Diego. And drew a lot of people; in fact we had to turn away 10,000 our first game in Los Angeles.

The Afro-Americans wanted to see their guys play against the white guys. And so they did. In Yankee Stadium the crowd was about 50-50; in Comiskey Park it might have been 60 to 70 percent black; in Los Angeles the same way, different towns; and San Diego maybe 50-50. Of course, in Vancouver not so much; in Seattle and Portland, we played two games in one day; we'd play over in Yakima in the afternoon, jump in the airplane. We had two airplanes, a DC-3 for both of us. And they were flown by the pilots of the Flying Tigers, the Flying Tigers Airlines.

I pitched twenty-six consecutive days. After pitching 36 complete games in 1946, I pitched twenty-six consecutive days, three innings or more, every night or every afternoon. I had to throw pretty hard for one or two hitters, and ease up a little bit, and Satch would do the same. He didn't pitch quite as much as I did, but they had Chet Brewer, who was an exact clone of Bob Gibson, both of them great pitchers. Chet Brewer from Des Moines, Iowa, and he was a great pitcher for the Monarchs, and a good friend of mine. They were all good friends of mine.

Jackie Robinson played three games against us. He played in Los Angeles, San Diego, and Sacramento. Jackie was not a great high fastball hitter; he was a good curveball hitter; he was a great base runner; and of course he did have his problems, how bad they were, how good they were, I don't know.

I knew they were going to bring up Jackie Robinson from Montreal. But I did know that blacks could play baseball, I'd known that ever since I was a kid in Des Moines, Iowa, playing all over Des Moines. Van Meter is only eighteen miles out of Des Moines; they had some good black players in Des Moines. I didn't really give it that much thought. Like I say you can either play or can't play. Some are overestimated; some are underestimated.

One of the best Afro-American or black, I use both terms all the time, was Joe Rogan. He could do anything; he could pitch; he could play infield; he could hit; he could catch; he played outfield; he's a good hitter. He was one of the best black ballplayers I ever saw, maybe just as good as Jackie.

Josh Gibson couldn't hit a curveball with an ironing board.

Josh Gibson

Yeah, I remember he had a lot of power; he could hit a fastball from here to Toledo, but he couldn't hit a curveball with an ironing board. Not a good curveball. He didn't see any fastballs off of your friend Feller, just that big, what we called epileptic snake.

Buck O'Neil always says that they won most of the games. I say to Buck, "Look, Buck, sssh, I got the scorebook." We don't talk about that. We were interested in one thing, making money. I mean what else is there; yes we put on a good show; there was racial rivalry, not amongst the players, but amongst the fans. And we got a few laughs, they're great friends of mine. They love me dearly, I love them dearly, I knew all the guys. We made more money in that month of October than we made all year round.

As a pitcher I had a very good curveball. I had very good control of my curve. I could throw strikes with my curveball no matter what the count was—3-and-nothing. I probably got half my strikeouts that year on curveballs because I'd throw the curveball anyhow, 3-and-nothing, 3-and-2. I could throw it over the plate—I'd say what percentage of the time—9 of 10. Besides that the plate is wider when you throw a curveball. A lot more hitters will swing at bad curveballs when they wouldn't swing at a bad fastball. In other words, it makes the plate that much bigger and the strike zone much larger because they'll swing at a curveball in the dirt or either right- or left-hand hitters, and a fastball they'd be taking it so therefore you've got a wider plate and a bigger strike zone.

I practiced bunting. I was a very, very good bunter. I'd get the man over a very large percentage of the time. Even if it was down the first baseline, the third baseline, no matter if it was a fastball, curveball, knuckleball, I could bunt very, very well and if I get two strikes on me with a left-hand pitcher on the mound, I might just lay a bunt down with two strikes. If it stayed fair, I was on first base, if it was foul, I'd go to the dugout.

I was never worried too much about getting paid on the number of hits I got. No, I was a pitcher—my batting average was .151 and I had quite a few extra base hits. I hit up the alley. I hit to right center quite a bit and two base hits if I got on the ball. I'd had eight home runs, which wasn't exactly going to break any records and I'm not a good curveball hitter. That's the only reason I became a pitcher, I couldn't hit the curveball so I decided I could throw better than I could hit.

In my opinion, today's pitchers don't throw enough. They don't throw enough, and I don't think they do the right physical exercises. The day after I pitched, I'd play pepper and shag balls in the outfield, throw a little bit. And I'd work real hard the next day. I'd do a lot of running, wind sprints, 100 yards or 90 yards, all-out, twenty, twenty-five times. Maybe pitch ten or fifteen minutes of batting practice, if the manager didn't ask me to go to the bull-pen and save me, might want to pitch to a hitter or two, or an inning. And then I'd rest the next day; I'd just break a sweat and loosen up, and do a lot of stretching exercises, a lot of calisthenics. The same thing I did aboard ship, twice a day, when conditions permitted, for the battleship *Alabama*, because it keeps the officers and the enlisted men in good condition.

Hank Greenberg couldn't hit me at all, but Tommy Henrich could hit me with his eyes closed at midnight and the lights out. There was about a dozen left-hand hitters, but Tommy Henrich— he and Johnny Pesky and some of them you may have never heard of.

Mostly, DiMaggio was the only right-hand hitter that bothered me. I didn't have a sinkerball and he couldn't hit a sinkerball pitcher like Bob Lemon. DiMaggio wanted the ball away from him, the big wide stance, and he couldn't move if you pitch him inside where you should.

Ted Williams and I had what you call a Mexican standoff. He'd get his hits; he'd get his home runs. He never got a home run from 1939, '40, and '41. All the years before the war he never got a home run but he got 10 after the war before he retired. I retired in '56. He played for several seasons longer. But Ted was the best hitter I ever saw. He didn't swing at any bad pitches. As soon as I saw Ted swinging at pitches that were not strikes, I knew he was in the sunset of his career and he knew that, too.

Ty Cobb used to come to Tucson to visit in 1947 and he visited with Hornsby and Tris Speaker, who were friends of his, and I had a beautiful picture taken with Ty Cobb, Hornsby, and Tris Speaker, the four of us. I was in uniform.

Larry Doby came up [in 1947] and of course I'm sure—Larry was a little uptight and understandably so. You see, the same as if I were joining the Kansas City Monarchs. And Larry was suspicious of people, that we didn't want him around, which was not true, at least as far as I was concerned anyway. I didn't know what the rest of the fellows thought. Didn't care. None of my business.

They're your own personal thoughts. Of course he couldn't stay in our hotel in '48 in Tucson. He had to stay in the rooming house. I know Larry was a little upset. He said some of the fellows didn't shake hands with him. He was introduced to us in Comiskey Park [in 1947]. I paid very little attention. Shook hands, said hello, welcome to the wigwam or some comment such as that and went about my own business. That is doing my own pitching, and doing my own thing and getting ready for another barnstorming tour against Satchel Paige's All-Star team.

Satchel Paige got there enough to help us a lot [in 1948]. He won a few ball games for us. He was six and one or seven and one. He was a great pitcher then. He lost his fastball about '49, even though he won some major league games when he pitched for the Browns later on and he got a little suspicious of his fastball. It wasn't doing very much and he hadn't that much of a curveball. He was a control pitcher and he was only a one-pitch pitcher. Even though he liked to throw the curveball, it broke only about that much but he had changes of speed that were beautiful. He could throw the ball through a keyhole and did.

And when I think going back all the way, to me, the color of a ballplayer meant nothing to me. Can you hit, run, throw, pitch? If you can do that, you belong here. They should have been there in 1839.

In 1948 we had several players having career years, like Dale Mitchell and Larry Doby and Ken Keltner and Joe Gordon and Jim Hegan, and Bob Lemon pitched very well. I couldn't beat anybody the first half of the season. Well, I won 10 of my last 12 starts and the biggest game of my career in that year in 1948 was beating the Red Sox on Don Black Night.

Don Black was a pitcher who had an aneurysm at home plate and almost died right there in the clubhouse on the rubbing table. He broke a blood vessel in his brain and just about died. Never was any good after that and he's a good friend of mine. So I pitched Don Black Night. All the money went to Don Black for his medical bills. I beat the Red Sox that night. That put us into a tie for first place. And I pitched the last game of the season against Newhouser, who pitched very well—pitched one of the best games of his career. Beat me, I mean, just beat me three days later over in Detroit just after that game in Cleveland against the Red Sox. That was the biggest game in '48 for me beating the Red Sox on Don Black Night. We went into a tie and we tied the Red Sox and went over there and beat them that particular game the next day in Boston.

Bill Veeck made one mistake, which he never should have done. I knew he was going to bring up Eddie Gaedel, that midget, up to bat. I knew he was going to get some attention. He got a lot of attention. He got too much attention. I mean that was an insult to the game of baseball.

He was in desperation. You know, of course, you're going to make mistakes. What I'm saying is, if you make a lot of big decisions, you're going to make some big mistakes. If you make no decisions at all, you're going to make no mistakes. That's the way it is.

Nineteen fifty-four was such an unusual year. We had very good starting pitching. We had good relievers and we had the left-hander relief pitcher named of Don Mossi who threw very hard, had a good curveball. Our fastball pitcher was Ray Narleski and we had Bob Hooper and Dave Hoskins and Hal Newhouser, who won six or seven games, only lost one or two, at the end of his career.

And let's see, I think it's Bob Hooper I'm trying to think of. And we had excellent starting pitching. We had George Strickland at short and Bobby Avila played second from Veracruz, Mexico. He led the league in hitting that year; hit .341, and Vic Wertz at first and, of course, Hegan had a good year catching. Al Rosen had a great year at third base, Doby and Bob Kennedy in the outfield as well.

Maybe Bob Kennedy wasn't there. We had Larry Doby and Dale Mitchell and had Dave Pope played right field part of the time. And who were the other—

Suitcase Simpson, maybe, maybe not. Not much. He came there in '51 I know. And Easter was there too, but he wasn't there in '48. Wertz was first base most of the time. Vic Wertz was a very powerful left-hand hitter; hit the ball that Willie Mays caught in the World Series in the opening game. We won 111, which was the most games since the Cubs won 116 back in what—1906 or 1908.

And the Yankees won 103 and weren't even close really. And then we go into the Series, and I did not pitch. I won 13 and lost 3 [that season]. I was pitching every other Sunday it seemed like, spot pitching. Durocher did a great job of managing the Giants. They had Johnny Antonelli and Sal Maglie and Marv Grissom, Don Liddle and their pitching staff was very good.

Johnny Antonelli pitched the best ball that I have ever seen a pitcher pitch in a short series. He was almost unhittable. That was, by far, the best postseason series he ever had. And they beat us. They were hot. Dusty Rhodes hit every time he swung a bat; he got a base hit or a home run. And you couldn't get him out. Durocher was very smart in his managing. Of course, Al Lopez couldn't do much about it. We lost the first game in 10 innings on a bloop home run by Rhodes that traveled about 252 feet.

I think it's 251 or 250 right down the line. And he hit perfect in a perfect spot. The next day he hit one off of Early Wynn. This was a legitimate home run. It was a 400-footer-plus. And our hitting: We were in a batting slump. We came to Cleveland and we played four straight days; no time off to travel. And the Giants, they flew in on an airplane and we just took a train and got in here and went right from the terminal right over to the ballpark and started playing.

The Giants got here the night before and got a good night's rest. We lost the next two games; our defense fell apart. Bob Lemon pitched with two days' rest and he pitched the last game and lost it.

We had Lemon; Garcia pitched the third game. And I was in the bullpen, but I did not pitch. We had a good ball club. The Giants were hot. Everything they did was right; everything we did didn't turn out so well. I think it had very little to do with the managing but they were hot and we were in a slump. And they deserved to be the world champs.

The 1948 team was a better ball club for one reason: We had better cohesion. We had a better leader in the lineup [in Lou Boudreau]. You have to have a good leader in the lineup. Not only on the bench with a good manager, you must have a good leader in the lineup [like Boudreau]. That's one of the big problems with the major league ball clubs today. Nobody in the lineup, or very few of them, want to take the responsibility of being a team leader. There's no money in it of any consequence. So nobody wants to be the team leader.

[In 1954] Al Rosen was the team leader in those days, the third baseman. Our third baseman had a very good year. And he had a good year in '55. Al was a very good hitter. Not a great third baseman, he had one good year defensively. Most of them were very mediocre but he was an excellent hitter, an excellent team man, a good man to have in the clubhouse and in the lineup between the white lines to lead the ball club. And if you don't have a good leader, no matter what business you're in, whether it's baseball or politics or any corporation or any business, if you don't have a good leader that you respect and you have to have cohesion like in the military. If you don't have cohesion, you're going to lose. And that goes for sports, too.

I liked Casey Stengel personally when you sit down to talk to him over a cup of coffee, the two of you. He was as normal as can be. As soon as he sat down on the bench with the news media around him, he'd tell all those double-talking stories. And the Yankee players hated it. They didn't like to listen to it. DiMaggio and Mantle, they couldn't stand Stengel even though they respected him. And I knew Casey Stengel before he was a genius, when he was a genius, and after he was a genius. He was no genius anymore, depending on the kind of ballplayers you have.

I thought Casey was a great person as a person. As a baseball manager I thought he was a good man. He knew how to handle the players but as far as being a great manager, I'll take Durocher anytime.

But Babe Ruth was a hero of mine. He was a great hitter, a great base runner, outfielder; he could throw to the right base. He had a great arm. He was a great pitcher, would have been if he didn't turn out to be a hitter where it was more money in hitting than pitching.

He was fun and he was all right. He didn't drink and dissipate as much as everybody said he did. He did a lot of darn fool things like everybody does when they're young. Of course, the old saying goes—my father had all these clichés—you can only be young once, but immature forever. Babe was a little that way but not too much. He liked show business; he enjoyed being in the limelight. He liked the photographers and the writers and the publicity and he was a pretty good con man. Like when he hit the home run in Chicago at Wrigley Field.

We all know that he was pointing into the dugout and not in center field, which doesn't mean anything. It was a good story and Babe realized it was a good story. And right away when they said, "You called the shot," he said, "Yes, I did." Well, he was pointing in the dugout, not center field.

In 1962, I was inducted into the Hall of Fame along with Jackie Robinson, Bill McKechnie, and Eddie Roush. That was one of the big days in my life and always will be. I'm the senior member of the Hall of Fame now. It's date of induction, not age. Because others are in their nineties and born long before I was but not inducted long before.

I came from a small farm—well, a large farm out in the center of Iowa, amongst the cornfields, loved America, loved to play sports, baseball, basketball. Had a great father, a great mother, and great managers and coaches. I was lucky.

The good Lord gave me the ability and the assistance from my coaches and managers. I was in the service, helping my little bit to maintain the sovereignty of the United States of America. When it's all over and all said and done, probably I'd like to have you just remember me as a good American, or an American that did what he thought was right. When the time came to either fish or cut bait, I joined the Navy three days after Pearl Harbor and went to war.

Came back and played eleven years of baseball. Had a great life. Been very lucky. I owe baseball a great deal. It's been very good to me. And I hope all you baseball fans, at this particular date in time, continue to support the game. And I hope the game is somewhat now like it was when I played, from 1936 to 1956.

TOMMY HENRICH

Thomas David Henrich was his name, but "Old Reliable" was more than a nickname for this longtime outfielder with the New York Yankees. Henrich was reliable, especially in a big spot.

After being granted his free agency from the Cleveland Indians by Commissioner Kenesaw Mountain Landis because he was being illegally "hidden" in the minors, Henrich would sign with the Yankees and spend his entire 11-season big league career, from 1937 to 1950, in pinstripes, missing three years (1943–45) while serving in the Coast Guard during World War II. As part of one of the Yankees' greatest outfield trios of all time, along with Joe DiMaggio in center and Charlie Keller in left, Henrich was a left-handed pull hitter with power, renowned for his leadership skills, steady play, and clutch hitting. And he was a five-time All-Star, leading the league in runs once and triples twice. But numbers cannot tell the true story of Henrich's importance to the team.

When DiMaggio, who once called Henrich the smartest player in the big leagues, was once asked why Henrich was nicknamed Old Reliable, he said, "His ability to make an outstanding catch, spark a rally, or drive in a key run when it counted." In presenting Henrich its 1949 Athlete of the Year award, Sport Magazine described him as the finest example of the modern ballplayer—quick-thinking, intelligent, moderate in his habits, and personally likable. And New York Times sports columnist Arthur Daley once wrote: "He came pretty close in character and performance to being the ideal Yankee, presuming there ever could be such a thing."

Tommy Henrich

A key member of seven Yankee teams that would capture World Series glory, Henrich is best remembered for one particular play in October. In Game 4 of the 1941 World Series, Henrich fanned to apparently end the game. But the ball got by Brooklyn Dodgers catcher Mickey Owen, and Henrich raced to first, helping the Yankees eventually win the game and the Series.

Henrich himself may have summed up the rules of big league baseball best when he said, "Catching a fly ball is a pleasure. But knowing what to do with it after you catch it is a business."

WHEN I WAS IN THE SIXTH GRADE, the city of Massillon, Ohio, got a league together, all the sixth-grade teams. So we had a team and we were pretty doggone good.

I would say this: I was about the fourth power hitter. I would be down the fourth place on power at that time in the sixth grade. So we had a good ball club. Now where do I go from there? Played softball until I was nineteen. Enjoyed it 'cause it was playing ball and really enjoyed it absolutely. Our team broke up and some guy asked me, "Would you like to play hardball, Tom?"

I says, "Yeah, I'll give it a shot."

So in the first year I'm doing okay and the scout for the Detroit Tigers, he was O'Boyle, he saw me playing and I got two hits off of the guy that he was scouting from Canton, Ohio. I got two line drive hits off of him. In the eighth inning he says, "How would you like to play pro ball?"

The bottom fell out of me. "You kidding?"

So I switched teams immediately to one in closer to home where we had batting practice every night. I says, "I've got a lot of work to do." So I switched over there and at the end of the season, along the way, Bill Bradley, an old third baseman of the Indians, he's the scout. He sees me play and in the first time at bat I see this dumb outfielder, left field, he's playing it like I'm a right-handed hitter and the center fielder's over there and there's a spot over there.

I'm trying to punch it in there. And I wasn't that good at place-hitting yet. So I said, "You better hit the ball where you can hit it." So the next pitch I hit over the road for a home run. Bill Bradley comes over to the house and he said, "Would you like to play ball?"

I said, "Yeah!" So he was such a nice guy I signed with him. Billy Evans, the old umpire, was the general manager of the Indians at that time. That's how I started.

Oh when I was, let me see, eight years old, Babe Ruth went to the Yankees, 1920. And now no radio, no nothing, you still heard of Babe Ruth. This is a phenomenon coming on the scene in New York. And I said, "Boy oh boy that's for me." So from that day on I was rooting for the Yankees. That's how it got started.

I signed with Billy Evans in Cleveland and I had spring training in '34 in Zanesville. I hit .326, played every game, yeah. At that time I was twenty-one.

Our manager got us all together and wanted everybody's right name and age and so forth and you send it in to somebody. And there was a big table here and this guy, Bud Uhl, graduate of Ohio Northern, when they got around to him, he said, "He's a college graduate, he's a college graduate."

And he said he was twenty-one. I says, "You ain't that smart. Something's going on here, boy." So when it got around to me I wasn't born in 1913 anymore, I was born in 1916. That made me eighteen right here and that's where it started. Lefty Gomez is the only ballplayer that knew my right age. I said, "Don't you ever tell anybody that." And he never did and during our career every once in a while I tried to nail Gomez a little bit. And he'd look at me and say, "Be nice to me, boy."

My salary my first year with the Yankees was $5,000. I was declared a free agent you know. I played Class D in Massillon, Class C in Zanesville, Ohio, and Class 1A in New Orleans, was sold to the Milwaukee Brewers at that time, farm club of the Cleveland Indians. Okay? During the winter, I read, I was not elated about being bought by Milwaukee because I've had three darn good years and I hit higher each year and I said, "Here we go to another one." Well in the paper, the Milwaukee [club] says, "They can sell me to the Boston Braves." And at the same time, a week later, the Cleveland *Plain Dealer* got in there, "Henrich is being considered for a trade with the St. Louis Browns."

And I say, "Who in the heck do I belong to?" So now I tell my dad what I'm going to do. I'm going to write to Judge Landis. He says, "Why are you going to write to Landis?" I said, "Dad, as far as I know Judge Landis is the only guy in baseball that's on the side of the players." He says, "Well, if you feel that way go ahead."

So that night I wrote the letter that I'm going to send to Landis. I put it on the kitchen table. When Dad came through, he read it and he says, "I wouldn't change a word." That's my dad. That's what I sent to Landis and he got into the thing and declared me a free agent.

Yes the idea back of my letter was that I was in communication with an executive of the Indians and at the same time I'm supposed to belong to Milwaukee. I was pretty smart on this one. I said on purpose, "Could you have traded me to some ball clubs along the line, basically I want more money?" And he [the Indians' executive] said, "Well yeah."

Now here's the Indians admit that they have the right to trade me to somebody else or sell me when at the same time Milwaukee claims that they own me. I was the first guy. I was the first guy who wrote the commissioner. I know that.

Well I heard from eight ball clubs and the Yankees were one of them. Oh, the Yankees were following me with Milwaukee for two weeks with Johnny Nee, scout. And I never saw him. I never knew

Judge Kenesaw Mountain Landis

that. But when I'm a free agent he showed up in Massillon. And when I heard "New York Yankees," well it made a great impression right there. I still tried to get whatever I could but here comes my dad. Now he's going to be around.

This is on Friday and Saturday, and my dad said to Johnny Nee, he said, "I don't know what we're going to do, but before we do anything we'll contact you." And Johnny Nee said, "That's good enough for me." Okay? These are two gentlemen.

And Dad, and when I chose the New York Yankees, we went down and talked with them. And Dad said, "This is '37 now. They're world champs already in '36." Dad said, "Do you think you can make that ball club?" I said, "I don't know, Dad, but I'll tell you something. If I find out that I'm a good ballplayer, I don't want to be with the St. Louis Browns."

I got to New York the day before the opening of the season in '37. When I walked in that clubhouse and met these guys, I'll tell you it had a, I'm saying, a profound influence on my feelings. Gehrig comes over, cordially shakes hands, good luck. Tony Lazzeri, the same thing, Bill Dickey, Lefty Gomez, Charlie Ruffing, Frank Crosetti, Red Rolfe, George Selkirk, Jake Powell.

(Manager Joe) McCarthy didn't talk to me the first day. "Hello." That's all. But it was about two or three days, the clubhouse guy said, "Mr. McCarthy wants to see you." And I go in there, sit down, talk. We get acquainted there a little bit. So, we talked this over and oh yes, everything's fine. He says, "Do you drink?"

I said, "Jesus Christ, what a question that is?" So I told him the truth. I says, "Yeah, I like beer." I said, "My dad made beer, even home brew." And I said, "Yeah, I drink beer, that's all." Okay nice speech.

McCarthy says, "You know I've been in baseball for twenty-nine years and I've never heard a ballplayer admit that he likes the hard stuff."

But then I went over to New York. I didn't get in the game for two weeks. They shipped me over to Newark.

I was only in Newark for ten days. Seven games. For ten days I hit .444, everything I hit bounced through someplace.

Joe McCarthy

So then here's McCarthy. The Yankees got beat two games in Detroit. McCarthy comes into the clubhouse the next day with a snarl on his face and so on. He's like this and as he passed by, Roy Johnson, the half-brother of Bob Johnson, Big Bob from the Athletics, McCarthy heard Roy Johnson say, "What's that guy expect to do, win every day?"

Well McCarthy *did* expect to win every day and he got to his office and he phoned (General Manager) Ed Barrow, he says, "Get Johnson out of here." He says, "I don't want him around here anymore."

And Ed Barrow says, "Well who do you want to take his place?"

And he says, "Send me that kid from Newark." That's how I got back to the Yankees. I was the kid.

Lou Gehrig didn't lead by being talkative, I'll tell you that. No, he was a very quiet, reserved type of guy. The respect that everybody had, take a look at the record. That's all you had to know is how great a ballplayer he had been, and he's a live-and-let-live guy. And I, thank God—I think Lou liked me, because I got along fine with him and in short order.

Every time I faced a new pitcher, I went to him and, boy, he would give me the best advice he could, 'cause he found out what kind of a hitter I was, a fastball hitter. And being able to talk with Lou and having him take an interest in me, I never forgot that, because I felt very close to him. And he even kidded with me.

And I think that that's quite a compliment in itself, but, oh, I was telling you when we played in Chicago, we went to St. Louis with him in a slump. Now, we get over to Philadelphia he hit four line drives, 4-for-4. I said to Bill Dickey, "I haven't seen line drives like that in my life." He says, "Wait a while." He says, "You're only looking at soft line drives."

Lou guarded home plate on the level and especially the high pitches. Oh, somebody asked him one time, "How come you've never been thrown out of a ball game?" He never was, okay? Never. And he said, "Well, you gotta know how to talk to the umpires."

Bill Dickey. Oh, man, those two guys—their personalities were the same, and they were together all the time. Oh, that was beautiful. They were kinda silent, they were, but they really respected each other. Why not? Take a look at their records.

DiMaggio, his personality was introverted. He was a very confident guy, and he had more drive and more deep desire inside not to do anything wrong. You know the one game he played at first base, I never saw him sweat in my life like that. You know why? Because he was afraid he was going to make a dumb mistake, 'cause he didn't feel like he knew what to do at first base, and that bothered him.

I watch these guys today, and you see it many times, outfielders getting in each other's way and so forth. We had a system. If I wanted the ball, I called for it, and DiMaggio gave it to me. If I didn't call for it, get out of the way, because DiMaggio is gonna catch it. And it was as simple as that.

I went out a lot with, when (Joe) Gordon got there and, oh, I don't know, whoever came along. But it wasn't DiMaggio. And I never had lunch with or dinner with—just the two, Lou and Dickey, I was never in with them. No, there's nothing wrong with that. And DiMaggio, I remember going back in the cab, just Joe and I are in the backseat, and we get out at the Del Prado in Chicago. He goes his way. I go my way. Nobody said boo about are you gonna have dinner tonight. And there's nothing wrong with that.

Lefty Gomez did a lot for Joe DiMaggio, made him feel at ease in different situations. And, yeah, Joe was at ease when he's with Lefty. Lefty could kid Joe.

I loved Bill Dickey. He was smart. Bill Dickey was a smart baseball player. And in the first year—no, what year is it? '39—we beat

Bill Dickey

the Reds. And Paul Derringer's pitching. In the ninth inning it's a tied score.

We got a guy on. Ival Goodman made a mistake in right field, dropped the ball that he should've had, and Charlie Keller ends up on third base with nobody out. What do you do? DiMaggio's the next hitter. Well, it's easy. There was a place to put him. Put him there. Now, you've got a question. Do you want to walk Bill Dickey too, and then pitch to Selkirk?

Or do you want to pitch to Bill Dickey? Paul Derringer's the pitcher, and I'm watching like a hawk. I know what they got to consider here, and I'll tell you the truth. The first pitch he threw to Bill Dickey, Bill took for strike one. Looks like they're going to pitch to him, and I turned around. "Where's my glove?" The idea was this game's over, and I wanna have my glove for sure.

Next pitch, line drive to center field. It's all over. Bill Dickey, that's what I thought of Bill Dickey.

Art Jorgens, look that name up, third-string catcher. He was with the Yankees ten years. Oh, yeah, he pinch-hit for Bill Dickey once, and, you know, I always remember, he was the third-string catcher. He would catch batting practice, and I remember I'm up there somehow or another, I'm not serious about it. Jorgens told me, "Knock it off, Tom. Get down to work here." And I'd sober up in a hurry. That's what they were. That's why they won.

I played for three prominent managers, Bucky Harris, Casey Stengel, and Joe McCarthy. I'll just plain put McCarthy in number one. That's all there is to it, and Casey Stengel is a very—never mind his way of talking. He knew the game of baseball as well as anybody, but his personality didn't fit in. I don't think DiMaggio liked him, Casey Stengel.

The attitude changed, of course, when you lose a McCarthy. Then we went through two years of Bucky Harris. Now, Bucky's a nice guy, but he didn't command the respect that McCarthy did.

When McCarthy left, Bill Dickey managed. Then they hired Bucky Harris. And Harris was fired after the '48 season. [General Manager George] Weiss fired Bucky Harris for being too lax. That's what they said. Now, I liked Bucky Harris, but I'll give you one for instance. I'm coming up in about the eighth inning against Washington. Mickey Vernon is playing first base and there's a situation where there's a man on first and second, nobody out. Is he going to have me bunt or not?

I don't want to bunt. And I went back to Bucky Harris and says, "What do you want me to do?" You know, I'm asking him bunt or not. He says, "Do what you want." McCarthy never would've said that. I believe he just never would've said that. He would've told me the way he wanted it done.

You respected Joe McCarthy, I'll tell you that, boy. You're a player, you respect that man. He didn't tell you to. You just did it. That's the way it was, and his personality commanded respect. That's because he knew the game. I don't know anybody that knew the game better than McCarthy. Oh, here's one for you. Ted Williams.

Fourth of July, 1939, Gehrig had sat down. And now they were going to honor him. When he got up to the microphone, I'm saying, "What can Lou say?" I mean, what is he capable of saying? And he was very serious about it. And, you might have seen tears in his eyes, I don't know. But, that's the way it was coming out.

The symptoms were apparent his first day in spring training. But nobody believed it. What's wrong? Nobody knows what's wrong. For heaven's sakes, he was having trouble getting out of the way of batting practice pitching. Pitch inside, he couldn't maneuver his body to get out of the way of it.

So it was just, just a plain old mystery. Nobody knows anything about it, but it was right there. So, and, it wasn't there in 1938, in the World Series. So, it happened over the wintertime. Whatever happened. I'm convinced of that.

Boy, that was a solemn deal. Especially when he says, I consider myself the luckiest man in the world. What in the world, everybody knew by that July. When he stopped playing, he did come and sit on the bench for a while.

I remember when Ruth and Gehrig embraced. And, it was, you would say, heartfelt. Because these guys had been separated for a

Lou Gehrig's farewell speech

couple of years. And, they were on the outs with each other. And, when they got down to the nitty-gritty, the Babe came over, boy.

Nineteen forty-one World Series. Game 4 ninth inning, and the Yankees are down a run, 4-to-3, but up in the series two games to one. The count is 3-and-2, and the pitch comes in. It's high, but now it starts to break. And I said, well, you'd better guard home plate. Not that I'm going to get a home run out of this thing, but I have to swing, because it's going to be a strike. And as I start to swing, I get out in here. That ball kept going.

And, before I get up here, I'm trying to put the brakes on, 'cause it's going too low. And I can't. I can't. I get all the way around here, I'm trying to bring the thing back. Larry Goetz, the umpire, says strike three. I knew it was strike three. But when I'm up here now, this is, how do you do that? How do you know how a brain works? Maybe Mickey Owen, the catcher, is having trouble, the same trouble I had.

Sure enough, when I got up here, I'm looking right now, there goes that ball. The ball went all the way to the, practically the dugout.

I reach base on a strikeout, passed ball. DiMaggio hit a bullet to left field. Here's a real good quiz question. Who was playing left field for the Dodgers? Ain't nobody knows. And, it's a one-hopper. So, I can only go to second base. Okay. Up comes Charlie Keller. The pitcher, Hugh Casey's, got strike two on him, and all he's doing is guarding home plate. There's two outs. And Charlie hit a fly ball to right field.

Not well hit, but in Ebbets Field, you don't have to hit them very hard to reach that wall. Now, I think this is the proof of that. This is a lazy fly ball, and it hits the chicken wire, which is above the concrete in right field. And the chicken wire, it hits there, and comes straight down. Now, the concrete is about that thick.

I think the ball hit up there, and then came down, and that enabled Joe DiMaggio to score from first, on a ball that I thought would have been caught in right field. But the lapse, the lazy fly in the first place, I delayed about two seconds. That meant, I'll tell you, I score, easily.

And I'm here, and Joe's coming in there. And, boy is he coming, boy he is really coming hard. They don't know where the ball is, he doesn't care. I know where home plate is. And he was always a hard slider. DiMaggio's coming in there. And he hit home plate. And, I think he carried about that far past home plate. Just to be in there.

So, now we're ahead 5-to-4. So, Keller's on second base. So, they don't want to pitch to Bill Dickey. [They walk him.] Not a bad move. Except, Joe Gordon is the next hitter. And he hit .500 against the Dodgers that series. Nobody else had that good a series. Gordon had a good series. Now, he hits a ball to left field, over the left fielder's head, and the left fielder was so inept, the ball is coming here, he turns around, and the ball came back this way, and this guy's over here. And the ball gets by him. And Bill Dickey, not a fast runner. And the ball is rolling toward the infield now. That's time. And that gives Bill Dickey a chance to score, all the way, not even a play on him at home plate. The question is, who was the left fielder? Would you believe that they had a guy that was a first baseman playing left field? Jimmy Wasdell.

Nineteen forty-one was the year of DiMaggio's streak. I don't think we made much of it. Yeah, the 20s, he's done that before. And the, or even the 30s, I don't know whether he had done that ever before. But, I will tell you, that, about the time he hit 35, this is getting pretty darn serious. Because, the record is only 44. So, we'd probably got into it, we were probably concerned earlier than 35.

Joe DiMaggio

At any rate, he's up to 38, and we're playing St. Louis, Elden Auker is the pitcher. In the 38th game, we're ahead 4-to-2. In the last of the eighth inning, DiMaggio's going to be the fourth hitter, and he doesn't have a hit yet. And I got a brainstorm. I said to myself, "All I got to do, if we get a guy on, and then I hit into a double play, there goes the streak."

I was hitting third. I went into the dugout while they're pitching to Red Rolfe, he's the second hitter. Johnny Sturm is already out. And I said to Joe McCarthy, "Joe, if Red gets on first base, is it okay for me to bunt?"

McCarthy thought about three or four seconds. In other words, he's thinking, what's the situation? And he says, "That'll be all right."

In other words, with Joe D's records and so forth, that's a pretty good play. Sure enough, Rolfe got a base on balls. I bunted off Auker. DiMaggio comes up, and the second pitch, a blue dart into left center field. So, the streak is still going.

When he tied George Sisler's record in Washington, this guy stole his bat. We found that out because the next game, the first inning, I'm ready to go up to hit and DiMaggio's coming up. And this is true. I'm going up to hit and I hear this voice, "Tom!"

I turn around and it's Joe. I says, "What?"

He says, "You got my bat."

And I said, "No."

He says, "Let me see it." And I walked over. I used the Joe DiMaggio model.

But he could see that's not the one he's been using for a month. And he says, "Somebody stole my bat." So I got on, then he went up. He hit a ball. It's true. He hit a line drive to right center field. The guy ran across, made a good decent catch on it. One out. Later, when I passed DiMaggio, he's going to the center and I'm going to right field. This is how I know whether he was worried. He says, "If it had been my bat, it would have been in there." So he's disgusted with the bat that he used. And I said, "Joe, look at mine, look at mine."

And he admitted that it felt pretty good. They give me another, and he used my bat before the thing was over. He got the base hit that broke the record. So he held on to the bat. Some Italian boy from Newark stole the bat in between ball games but nobody knew it. Now, during the week they find out that that kid in Newark has got Joe DiMaggio's ball bat.

And some of the Italians over there said, "This bat's going back to Big Joe." So they got the bat from this kid, gave it to Joe. And then he stopped using mine and went back to his own and he went on from there.

I don't know what year I got the nickname Old Reliable. I know the first I ever heard of it, I think that it was said, we were playing in Philadelphia. We were one run ahead, ninth inning, two men out. The batter hit a pop fly, foul, and our catcher, Kenny Silvestri, didn't catch the ball. Next pitch, home run. Now the game's tied. We go into extra innings.

Rizzuto's the first hitter, he gets a single. I come up, put on the hit-and-run with Phil. He's starting out and I punch the ball into the left field corner. And the guy had some trouble out there because Rizzuto went all the way from first to home. It wasn't even close. So now we're ahead right away. And on the radio Russ Hodges says, "Old Reliable. He does it again."

In 1941 Phil Rizzuto joined us, he and Gerry Priddy. They're bringing them up together, Gerry Priddy and Phil. McCarthy got a brainstorm. He got rid of Babe Dahlgren because he said his arms were too short. That's what he said. I never knew of short arms before. I don't know why he didn't like Babe Dahlgren.

Anyway, he figured, I'll put Joe Gordon on first base, Priddy at second, Rizzuto, boom. Now, we got a great infield. But Priddy isn't performing very well. But Phil is. So this game—and here's McCarthy—Priddy must have made another error and as he comes in, apparently some guy is heckling him. And he comes into the bench and he's mad.

He sits down next to Phil and they're both sitting about five feet away from McCarthy. That's on that end. McCarthy had always sat there. It was always enough room around him, too. But Phil and

Gerry are like that. And McCarthy hears Gerry Priddy saying, "Dog-gone that son of a gun up in the stands," he says. "I'd like to get my hands on him."

And Phil says, "What's he like, Gerry? Has he got black hair?"

He says, "Yeah, he's got black hair."

"Kind of curly?"

"Yeah, it's curly."

He says, "Has he got a black mustache?"

He says, "Yeah."

Rizzuto says, "That's my dad."

McCarthy heard that and he says, "That little dago's got it." And he did have it.

I was in the Coast Guard. And I'll just say that, my opinion, Bobby Feller wouldn't admire this, but, I hate war. And I would say I was lucky. I was in the Coast Guard, and I was in Sault Sainte Marie, a couple years. I had a perfect record in the service—I went in as a specialist, first class, and thirty-seven months later, I came out, specialist first class.

In World War II you put Feller at the top of the list of ballplayers. He's the guy that enlisted.

I've always said that on real good ball clubs, there's usually a guy that you can lean on a little bit, and that's what Hank Greenberg was to the Tigers. He was big, he was important, and they could lean on Greenberg. Of course, what he did with a ball bat was, what I saw, it was remarkable. And I loved Hank, I thought he was a great guy. And I got pretty close to him.

I have a Joe DiMaggio and Hank Greenberg story. Johnny Murphy is in, pitching in relief already. It's about the eighth inning, ninth inning. It's the ninth inning. At that time, you walk through center field, exit, to get, the bullpen was beyond. You walk past the center fielder. Murphy is passing Joe DiMaggio.

And DiMaggio says to Murphy, "Why don't we fast-ball this guy once? You know, everyone is curving the son of a gun; don't curve him." Well, Murphy's curving, because that's the kind of a pitcher he was. So, from center field to the mound, Murphy says, that might be a good idea.

So, he fast-balled Greenberg. Home run. The game's over. Now, in the clubhouse. No sound. We're in there. We got beat. DiMaggio's over there, Murphy is here, and I'm over on this side. And about less than five minutes, DiMaggio stands up, and goes over to Murphy and says, "Don't you ever listen to another word I say."

I know Greenberg took a lot of abuse for being Jewish. The Yankees never said anything to him. Not a word. Not one word. I think the only time, the only thing I ever heard was the White Sox did. And he stopped them. I understand that they were getting on a Jewish topic. And he heard it. Greenberg went into the Chicago clubhouse and confronted them. And he said, "Which one of you is the guy that's saying this, which one of you? Stand up." Nobody stood up.

I don't know whether he could fight a lick, but he scared the bejeebers out of them. The way he was feeling, I would have thought he would have been a pretty fair fighter.

I admired Charlie Gehringer. He was so rhythmic. He was so smooth in all he did, that nothing looked tough. He was such a great ballplayer. I don't know whether to say that he was even a better hitter than he was a second baseman. That makes him pretty good. Because, with a bat in his hand, I don't know what he hit. Old Lefty Gomez says, "Oh, he makes me sick."

He says, "He goes to spring training, he gets a piece of chalk, goes over, writes a number on the board, then goes out and hits it." So, we had a lot of respect for Gehringer, and a nice, smooth guy. Never, never said boo to you. But, he was really, if he's the best, it's not a bad pick, I'll say that.

As a second baseman, I'm not sure how good Jackie Robinson was, as second baseman. I really am not that sure. To me, where he was a standout was the rest of him. He was not a good-looking hitter, but he was a good hitter. He didn't look good. He didn't have a rhythmic swing like Gehringer did. That doesn't make any difference. Where's the ball going? And when he got on base, jeez, scare the daylights out of you. I don't know, I saw him, he's on third base, it's an exhibition game in Brooklyn. Allie Reynolds is pitching. And I swear to you, Jackie is running down the third base line. And he's way down under here, and he doesn't steal home.

He goes back. And I saw him bouncing around over there so much, and Reynolds didn't know what to do about it. I said, "Jeez, he scares the daylights out of you. What's he going to do?" That's how, a lot of infielders played that way against Jackie. Tough guy. Boy, I'll tell you. I admired him. He took it. Boy, did he take it, from the white guys, before he got there.

People say, what's your first, when was the first time you were near him? I said, World Series, '47. He was a first baseman that year. And I got on base, and people say, what'd you say? I says, "I didn't say hello to him, and he didn't say hello to me." "If they want to know why," I said, "Hey, this wasn't a tea party."

So that's how it goes. At the time, I admired him. I know what he's been through. George Selkirk was a manager at Jersey City. And he says, "Tom, he earned his way up, boy, what we did to him last year." So, there I got the proof, what the white guys did, about Jackie Robinson.

Joe Gordon was absolutely one of my favorite guys because his attitude on a ball field, you see, was right made to order for Joe McCarthy.

I'm going to tell you something. I don't know why, maybe it's because I was playing against Cleveland, but, I had a lot of success against Bob Feller.

In 1949 Johnny Mize played some first base, yeah. But the pitching was Vic Raschi, Allie Reynolds, and Eddie Lopat, and that isn't bad. (Well, we get down to the end of the season.) The Red Sox got in first place when they were playing us. And in the late innings, I'm playing first base, and Bobby Doerr he's going to bunt to get this guy in from third, Johnny Pesky.

And I'm playing first base and I notice Bobby. And I start running in. And he bunted toward me. I got the ball and I threw it to home plate to Ralph Houk and he's guarding home plate like a Sherman tank. He's right there, tags Johnny Pesky. And Bill Grieve called him safe, right? No way. I said the only way he could have got in there is if he come from underneath like a mole.

But they beat us because of that and they're in first place. And we got a week to go and they're down in Washington with a two-game lead. And the Sox lose the first game. I said, "Boy we got a shot at them." Now, they're only one game ahead and we're playing them two. And that's how that thing went down to the wire. The last game now—DiMaggio is in center field with the flu, with the flu. He's weak.

We're ahead 5-to-nothing. Raschi pitching and he walked Williams for one. Then they got a base hit. They hit a ball out to DiMaggio and he should have caught the ball and he can't move. He took himself out of the game. He took himself out of the game, because he knew he should have caught that ball. We put in Cliff Mapes in center field. Guy hit a fly ball and Mapes threw the ball to home plate.

Mapes, he was the best. He had a great arm and direction. Beautiful thrower. So it was not too deep for the guy at third to come in 'cause that isn't even a tying run. All right. Yogi (Berra) catches it at home plate. Raschi is backing up. I'm at the mound now and here comes Raschi. And Yogi's going to give him a pep talk and so am I. And the way Raschi walks, he comes out there and before we got a chance to say anything, he said to Yogi—I think I'm allowed this word—he says, "Give me the damn ball and get the hell out of here."

Well, I walked away and I said, "We're in, boy. (Birdie) Tebbetts ain't going to hit that bird." He hit a pop fly down the first base line. Jerry Coleman's going, "I got it, I got it."

I said, "The heck you have. This is mine." 'Cause I'm in foul territory and Jerry Coleman's calling the ball. And I was standing there waiting for it. I said, "Get out of here." So that's how we won the pennant. That was a very satisfying pennant race.

Then we faced the Dodgers in the World Series. We beat them 1-to-nothing in the first game and they beat us 1-to-nothing in the second game. And we went over there and one thing I remember. We built up a good lead in Game 5 and some of the young kids—I really remember saying this—some of the kids that are in there, they're fooling around already. You know, they're having some fun and Brooklyn hasn't given up. They got a couple of runs. And I remember looking. I says, "Knock it off."

I said, "This is the best chance we're ever going to have to win a World Series. Let's win this game." So they shut up in a hurry.

Well, I wasn't in the brain department for the Yankees but I would say that they didn't look with favor on having a Negro ballplayer. That's the way I felt. And, you know, you'd say, "When are the Yankees going to get a colored ballplayer?" And the answer was, "When the Yankees find one good enough." Well, they found one guy, Vic Power. Vic Power was the best defensive first baseman I ever saw in my life.

I live in Prescott, Arizona, you know. And I go down to the vets in the hospital. I went down and talked to, I don't know, oh, fifteen, twenty of the vets—you know, the guys in there the rest of their life. And they're baseball fans. And I got to know some of them. And I'm in there this one time and the guy says, "Tom, did you ever face Satchel Paige?"

I says, "Yes, I did. Yeah, I faced Paige."

And well, he says, "Listen to me." He said, "Do you know about that crazy pitch that he had?"

And I said, "Do you mean the hesitation pitch?"

He says, "Yeah. Yeah."

I says, "He threw it to me."

He said, "Is that right?"

You know, what he would do is he'd take a stride and then he'd throw the ball. And he pitched to me like that, okay.

He said, "What did you do?"

I says, "I hit it into the Cleveland dugout." Satchel was a real good guy, no dummy.

The Yankees signed a contract with United Airlines to be the first ball club that flew. In '46, I was a player representative. Last week, I get a piece of paper that says, "Get the ballplayers to read this and sign" or whatever.

It was permission for, they will fly next year. Well, there were only five guys that wouldn't fly; I was one of them. Next spring training, several guys including Charlie Keller, they don't want to fly. So they said, "Tom, you're the representative. Go in and talk to Larry McPhail."

So I go in, "This is what's going on in the ball club."

He says, "Tom, that's what I sent that piece of paper around for."

I says, "I know that. But they're just telling me this."

He said, "Let me see the list." He says, "Keller and Rizzuto?" He says, "Those two are flying for sure."

I said, "Why?"

He says, "I know about the plane that Bobby Feller provided for them for barnstorming games. If they'll go up in the air with Feller in that plane, they're going up in United Airlines."

I came back and I says, "You guys are out of business, boy, the way he gave me the facts."

There's no denying, ballplayers today are bigger, stronger, possibly faster. They're a complete athlete. You have more of them than we had, I think. That's my own impression when I see them. And what bothers me more than anything else, that turns my attention to anything but pro sports is that they're in love with money. Nothing wrong with getting all you could. We got as much as we could get, all right.

That part's okay. When it engulfs you, this is your whole deal, dollar bills with their agent—he's looking to improve your salary and so forth to the point where you are not putting out all your best on the playing field; and then you got an alibi for this, and you got an alibi for that—I have no regard for that.

Comparing today's ballplayers with the guys of my era, I'd say we're talking about guys with, I think on an average, more speed for running, and 95 miles per hour for pitching. That's not rare anymore. I heard Yogi and Jim Kaat say—this is about fifteen years ago—Yogi says, "Oh, hitting today"—he says, "Tell me a guy that's got a good curveball."

That's Yogi reaction. And Jim Kaat thought the same way, that the pitching isn't as good. And I watch these guys throwing these bullets, and I say, "Hey, that's pretty good stuff." There weren't very many guys when I was playing throwing that hard. But these guys—you got a lot of guys playing ball today with good swings. And the best one I think is Mark McGwire. Mark McGwire could've been a home run hitter any era of baseball.

Stan Musial said it gripes him when he sees frail infielders, shortstops, hitting inside pitches out of the ballpark to the opposite field. I says, "There's something wrong here." I don't mind Mark McGwire hitting the home runs. And a lot of guys today got very good swings. They really do.

There's another thing. With the doggone difference in the American and National League the designated hitter. And you got a guy (pitcher), he's not afraid to knock that guy (batter) down because he's never going to come to the plate. Now, I don't buy that at all today. And that goes on. I can see that. But pitching inside is an art. Sal Maglie could do it.

I got a tremendous thrill out of seeing in print—Red Smith, who I thought was the best writer in his time, he had in there a line about, "Tommy Henrich, I think, enjoys playing baseball more than any guy I've ever seen." And if any part of that is true, I feel very, very good about it, because I did enjoy playing ball. And it's been my whole life; that's all there is to it.

JOHN "BUCK" O'NEIL

John Jordan "Buck" O'Neil has spent his life in the game as a player, manager, coach, and scout, and he excelled at them all. His Negro Leagues debut came with the Memphis Red Sox in 1937. He became a top-flight first baseman and soon began a long tenure with the Kansas City Monarchs. After serving in World War II, he was named manager in 1948. He would win five pennants and two Negro Leagues World Series as skipper of the Monarchs.

"He was a good manager," said Alfred "Slick" Surratt. "He could tear you up, and after he had gotten through he'd pat you on the back and say, 'Now go out there and hit the ball like I know you can.'" Another Monarchs player, Elston Howard, said, "Buck helped me a lot. He knows baseball and is a gentleman all the way."

O'Neil left the Monarchs to become a scout for the Chicago Cubs, helping to sign Ernie Banks, Lou Brock, Joe Carter, and Lee Smith. Banks was very happy when O'Neil joined the Cubs: "He had seen me play when I was just starting and he would know when I wasn't doing things naturally. He's very observant. He can sit in the dugout and spot little things that you're doing wrong. And he tells you in such a nice way . . . sort of like 'please let me help you.'"

O'Neil would also serve as a scout for the Kansas City Royals, as a member of the Hall of Fame's Veterans Committee, and as chairman of the Negro Leagues Baseball Museum. But when he provided commentary in the 1994 Ken Burns's PBS documentary "Baseball," his national profile exploded.

"He's a great gift from baseball to the rest of the nation, he is the keeper of some very important memories about the Negro Leagues, and he has a quality of being that is as advanced and as generous and as inspiring as that of any individual I've had the great fortune to interview and get to know," said Burns. "He is wise, funny, self-deprecating, and absolutely sure of what he wants from life. He is my hero, my friend, my mentor. He is like Abraham Lincoln and Jackie Robinson, what human progress is all about."

And O'Neil holds no bitterness regarding his exclusion from big league baseball, saying, "Waste no tears for me. I didn't come along too early—I was right on time."

MY FATHER WAS A BASEBALL PLAYER. My father was a sawmiller and all the sawmill towns, they had a baseball team; and my father was on that team. And I was the batboy, I'd go around with them.

John "Buck" O'Neil

Always had good hands. I could catch the ball, even when I was this high. And the men would throw me the ball and I'd catch the ball. And oh, I was a ham, you know. And oh, they loved it. They'd throw me pennies and nickels and things like that. That's when baseball got—I become attached to baseball.

My uncle lived in New York. He was a railroad man. He came to spend a couple of weeks with us one summer. And I'm telling him about the great baseball players that I've seen, the greatest baseball players in the world. He said, "John."

I said, "Yes, sir."

"How do you know they're the greatest baseball players in the world?"

I said, "They're in the major league."

He said, "Well, then, I'll tell you what. I'm coming back this fall. I'm going to take you and your father down to West Palm Beach. I want you to see some other baseball players."

I said, "Yes, sir." Appease an old man, but I knew I had seen the best baseball players in the world. I'd seen Ruth; I'd seen Ty Cobb; I'd seen Walter Johnson, you know. Anyway, he came that fall and took us down to West Palm Beach. And over at Palm Beach, at the Royal Ponciana Hotel, Rube Foster and Chicago American Giants, they represented that hotel, played twice a week, Thursdays and Sundays. And over at the Breakers Hotel, another big tourist hotel, was C. I. Taylor, Indianapolis ABC's.

And so, before going down there—the *Tampa Tribune* was a great paper. And we got the sports section there, and the kids would come by my house and I'd spread the paper out in the backyard and we would talk about what had happened in the major leagues. I would probably emulate Babe Ruth; another kid would emulate Ty Cobb; another kid would go to Walter Johnson; this is what we did. Now, going to Palm Beach, over at the Royal Ponciana, that's Rube Foster.

Rube Foster had eight guys on that ball club, could steal you 30, 40, or 50 bases, could hit you .350 or better. It was a type of ball I'd never seen before because it was quick. See, Major League Baseball to me was this, you could go get some popcorn or soda, whatever you wanted to, until Ruth came up, or some of the big hitters would come up, some of the big stars. But with this, uh-uh. You couldn't leave because you might miss something you'd never seen before, because these guys, man, would steal second, steal third, steal home, if you wasn't smart.

And it was that kind of baseball. So when I got back to Sarasota, my uncle subscribed to the *Amsterdam News*—that was the New York City weekly. And my father subscribed to the *Pittsburgh Courier* and *Chicago Defender*. See, these are weeklies. We don't get the paper until around Tuesday. But Tuesday evening, everybody would come to my house and we'd spread these papers out in the yard.

Now, the guy—I would probably be Rube Foster; another guy would be C. I. Taylor; and so on. So because—and it gave me a hope that I never had before, because all of the guys that I'd seen making a living playing baseball, they were white. So now, this was a chance for me to make my living playing baseball. So that's it.

Well, actually a lot of people say to me now that, "I know you hated it because you couldn't play Major League Baseball." I'd say, "No. No. No." If I was going to hate, it would be, actually, I couldn't attend Sarasota High School. I couldn't matriculate at the University of Florida. That was, you know, 'cause I played, some of the best baseball that was played in this country. So that didn't hurt me as bad as the education part. Because I'm in Sarasota and 1924, they're building a brand-new high school, Sarasota High School.

I'm running around, "I'm going to Sarasota High School. I'm going to Sarasota High School."

My grandmother said, "Sit down, son."

I said, "Yes, ma'am."

She said, "You aren't going to Sarasota High School."

I said, "Why, Grandma?"

"Sarasota High School is for white kids." I cried. She said, "Don't cry, because one day all kids will be able to attend Sarasota High School." And I tell you what, three years ago, Sarasota High School gave me an honorary diploma.

Well, one thing I always did believe, and I was from a Christian family, and we just believed it's going to change one day. These things were going to change. And we lived in a way that it was hard, actually, to deny us. Because one thing, you're talking about hate; we should've been the one doing the hating, but we didn't. No. We didn't. We didn't hate. They always tell me now, they say, "Buck, I know you hate what people has done to your people or did to you." I said, well, I never learned to hate.

I hate cancer. Cancer killed my mother, and my wife died two and a half years ago from cancer. I hate cancer. I hate AIDS. A friend of mine, thirty-five years old, died of AIDS three months ago. I hate AIDS. I hate what the Klan would do. I hate what the Skinheads would do. I hate what a crooked politician would do. But I can't hate a human being.

Baseball actually was a social event in the black neighborhoods. It's a social time. Even when we played here in Kansas City. Church service: Unh-unh. When the Monarchs are in town, it's 10:00, so they could come to the ball game. And they came looking pretty. It was a social event. Yeah, you come; you're with your friends and you wanted to look your best.

I'm seventeen years old now—my father said, "You playing baseball every weekend with a young man named Hasley, and he went to Edward Waters College. He's teaching over there at Booker Grammar School. Why don't you talk with him? You're a good athlete; you might get a scholarship."

I said, "Okay." Call him—called Lloyd Hasley, told him what I want.

I get to Edward Waters. I get there, oh, man. And I got my high school, see, because in Florida at the time, there was only four high schools in the state of Florida for black kids—Miami, West Palm Beach, Jacksonville, and Tampa. So I got there, got my high school. Oh, man, got my high school, doing good. Got two years college, yeah, on that scholarship.

And some of the guys that played on the college team would go north every year and play ball in the summer. They'd say, "Man, you're a good ballplayer. Why don't you go north with us and play ball this summer?"

I said, "Okay." I went north with the Miami Giants, good semi-pro ball club. Went north and all the way into Canada. Had a good year, got back to Miami.

The man that ran the ball club said, "Hey, why don't you stay down here and play ball with us this winter?" They played ball year-round, see.

I said, "No, man. I got to go back to school."

He said, "You always talk about Ms. Booker. How much money does Ms. Booker make?"

I said, "Sixty dollars a month."

He said, "You made more money than that playing with us." He said, "You think about that."

I said, "Okay." I get to the rooming house that night. I call Mama. I said, "Mama."

"Yes, son."

"I want to stay down here and play ball this winter."

She said, "Boy, you got to go back to school."

I said, "Mama, I made more money than Ms. Booker."

She says, "Son, Ms. Booker can work on that job until she's seventy, if she cares to." She said, "But what you going to do when you're thirty-five or forty years old and can't play baseball any-more?"

I said, "Mama, let me talk to Papa." Knowing a man, he's on the farm, you know, and he's very proud of what I'm doing. His son hit a home run. He's reading the paper where I did this or did that, and he was proud of that.

He said, "I'll tell you son, you can stay this winter. Next year, you got to go back to school."

I said, "Yes, sir. All right."

Stayed that winter, had a good winter down there. Next summer, went north again. And get back in the fall, it's time for me to go back to school. When I get back to Miami, Adolph Luque was there waiting for me.

"I want you to come to Havana and play on my ball club. I'm going to pay you $400 a month and all expenses paid." That was the end of the education right there.

Of course it was a lot of money. A lot of money. See, actually, it's a myth because a lot of people don't realize—see, some of the Negro League ballplayers were making more money than major league ballplayers, because at the time, the minimum salary in the major leagues was $5,000. See. And the George Gibsons were making $1,000 a month playing over here, and he was going, making maybe $3,000 playing Cuba, Mexico.

Well, in baseball, this was outstanding baseball because the best Cuban ballplayers in the world was playing with and against the best Negro League ballplayers in the world. It was outstanding baseball.

Martin Dihigo

All you needed was a bus, a couple of sets of uniforms, and you could have twenty of the best athletes in the world playing.

I saw Martin Dihigo, might have been one of the best ballplayers that ever lived. See, he's in the Hall of Fame in South America. He's in the Hall of Fame in Cuba. He's in the Hall of Fame in Mexico. And he's in Cooperstown. Could play all the positions. See, when he wasn't pitching, he played outfield. He led the league in pitching and led the league in hitting. That was Martin—Martin Dihigo, great, great pitcher, great player. Adolph Luque. Gonzales. All of these guys, they're just outstanding baseball players.

In Cuba, Mexico, Puerto Rico, I was a baseball player. When I got back home, I was a black baseball player.

My daddy said, "Man, follow your dream. Follow your dream." He said, "You'll have some hard knocks, but it's going to turn out for you." And so I went to play with—of course, when we were in Louisiana, a guy named Winfield Welch; he ran the ball club there, that Shreveport Acme Giants. And he told me, he said, "Now, next year," he say, "why don't you come up here and play with me?" So I went to play with him, and they were like a farm team to the Monarchs, his team. So I went and played with them.

All right. And so I played with this ball club. And I stayed in Shreveport that winter. And the next spring, the Monarchs trained in Shreveport. So the owner, J. L. Wilkinson, and Andy Cooper, who was the manager, they liked me. And they said, "Why don't you come on and play with the Monarchs?" He said, "But I tell you what"—the man at first baseman, his name was Mayweather, Ed Mayweather. He broke his leg the year before. He said, "Now, I've got to give Mayweather a chance, you know, to see if he can come back. But I know I'm going to send you over to Memphis to play with the Memphis Red Sox." That's '37. So I played with the Memphis Red Sox one year. And then they traded Mayweather to St. Louis, so then I went in '38 to the Monarchs.

Satchel Paige was famous, but he became more famous with the Kansas City Monarchs because they wrote a story about Satchel Paige in *The Saturday Evening Post*. That gave him that notoriety. And see, Satchel hurt his arm. Satchel had hurt his arm in '37, playing in

Satchel Paige

the Dominican, someplace down there. He's hurt that arm. So then, he didn't have a job. And J. L. Wilkinson, 1938, J. L. Wilkinson saw the potential there, knew he was a great drawing card.

So what he did, he brought Satchel with us and he made another team, and sent Satchel and Newt Joseph, sent them out West; played in the West, all the way into Canada, all the way out to California. And we called them the Second Monarchs. But they played and Satchel pitched. Satchel was pitching but they would—this same guy, Winfield Welch, with the Shreveport Acme Giants, that team, they traveled around with them and they carried Satchel.

But when Satchel would pitch a couple of innings, he was a draw, you know. They really wouldn't hit the ball, you know. They'd hit the ball and—you know how they would do it, and really didn't bear down on it. We'd sent our trainer out there with Satchel, and he'd rub that arm of Satchel.

After they was out there about two months, he told Welch one night, he said, "Turn them loose."

He said, "What?"

He said, "Turn them loose. They don't have to hold out tonight." He struck out 17 that night.

Called Wilkinson, said, "He's ready to come back," so he came back to the Monarchs. He was a natural showman. He was just a natural.

You know the lights started in the Negro Leagues, J. L. Wilkinson, the Kansas City Monarchs, night baseball. See we had night baseball five years before you played that ball game in Cincinnati.

You have to think about Kansas City, though. And if you think about Kansas City, Kansas City was wide open, Pendergast era. Musicians flocked here because every—they could get a gig in Kansas City. Because the hotels had live music; the bars had live music; the theater had live music. So everybody was here. I'll tell you something that happened to me one night. See, after—see, downtown, everything closed say at 1:00. We had a club here on 18th and Vine; we called it the Subway. And these musicians would all gather at the Subway after 1:00 and jam—jam session. And when I was in town, man, I would go to the jam sessions, see, because I knew a lot of the guys. I'm sitting here with Count Basie this night. Count had played.

Here's a kid, came in with a horn. Yeah. And he started playing, didn't none of us know what he was playing, but you had to listen because you never heard it before. That was Charlie Parker. And I met so many musicians there. And like, the musicians, though, they followed baseball. Count Basie was a Yankee fan, see. And I was always betting against the Yankees. So every World Series, I'm betting on the Dodgers or somebody else. And he was betting on the Yankees. He would skin me, you know that. And but we had a good time doing it.

•   •   •

Yeah, Satchel was satisfied in the Negro Leagues, because Satchel was making more money than most major leaguers was making. Why he would pitch against the local team—like, when he would play with a Negro League team—he would pitch for a Negro League team, say you would give him 40 percent of the money. But there, when he pitched against the other ball clubs, those local ball clubs, he's getting 70 percent of the money. Yeah. Seventy percent of the money. And he always—Satchel always got that big cut, and everybody wanted to see Satchel play. So actually, Satchel took a pay cut going to the major leagues.

See, the white team had the Kansas City Blues, who was a Yankee franchise. This was Rizzuto and Hank Bauer, all of those guys came through here, Kansas City. But as far as the, you know, the black community, we were superstars. Yeah, everybody—yeah. Doctors introducing you to their daughters and they're asking you to dinner and things like that.

We came to town when the Blues left. We played in the same stadium.

World War II changed a lot of people's thinking. And then, what actually happened is, the white media, the New York papers, they started writing about these things, about the segregation, how unfair it was. They started writing. And then, Wendell Smith, with *The Courier*, he'd been writing all the time. Now the white writers start talking about it.

To me, the greatest major league ballplayer ever lived, to me, was Willie Mays. But the best baseball player I've ever seen: Oscar Charleston. Oh, you should've seen him. See, Oscar Charleston could steal you 50 bases. Oscar Charleston could hit you 35 or 40 home runs. Oscar Charleston—I'll tell you what the old-timers say. The closest thing to Oscar was Willie.

He was built like a—big chest, got a good chest. And neat in the waist. Must have weighed, say 190 pounds, about five-eleven. Yeah, great body. Great body. Could play.

We know about Satchel. But some of the other great pitchers like Leon Day, Bullet Joe Rogan, they were just—had great stuff and knew how to pitch. You had to know how to pitch. See, the

Oscar Charleston

majority of pitchers in the Negro Leagues were good athletes, period. Played other positions. See, Bullet Joe Rogan played the outfield when he wasn't pitching and hit in the fourth spot. That kind of guy.

Leon Day. Um hum. If he wasn't pitching, he played the outfield. Oh, man. Willie Foster. Willie Foster was a great left-handed pitcher. Luis Tiant. You know Tiant, father of the major leaguer. His daddy. Great screwball pitcher, left-hander. Um-hum. Slim Jones. Philly Stars, great left-hander. He and Satchel had duels together.

A lot of people thought when we would come to New York to play, we would leave Kansas City and go to New York. No. No. It might take us the month to get to New York. You know, we played our way. We played our way. If we're going to New York, now, we're going to play St. Louis; we were going to play Indianapolis; we were going to play Cleveland; we played our way all the way. Then we played on into Pittsburgh. Then we went over to Washington and Philadelphia, Newark, New York.

It wasn't like a lot people thought, we just left here on the bus and took that long trip, no. We played our way there. And it was outstanding. It was outstanding, see, because we had interleague play; two weeks out of the year, the teams—in the American League, that was Cleveland back to Kansas City—we would go east. And two weeks, they would come west. So everybody could see all of the teams. And oh, you're talking about some games.

And I remember playing. And see, my favorite ballpark is really Yankee Stadium. We'd play in that Yankee Stadium and we got people all over there. I remember we'd go into the Yankee Stadium; we were staying at the Woodside Hotel. The first time I ever rode in a Rolls-Royce might be the last time. I don't ever remember I was in one again. Bill Bojangles Robinson was a part-owner of the New York Black Yankees. I rode from the ballpark back to the hotel in his Rolls-Royce. Yeah, that was something.

Oh, Cool Papa Bell just about as fast as anybody that ever ran. And Satchel said Cool Papa was so fast he could cut out the light and get in bed before the room got dark.

Josh Gibson. Great catcher. Great power hitter. See, they talk about now, like, McGwire and Sosa. Good hitters, great power hitters, but Josh Gibson, not only a great power hitter, he was a great hitter. They had .350 or better lifetime batting average. They were great hitters, not just power.

When Branch Rickey signed Jackie Robinson to that contract, that was the beginning of the modern-day civil rights movement. That was before *Brown vs. the Board of Education*. Mm-hmm. That was before Sister Rosa Parks said, "I'm tired today. I ain't going to the back of the bus." Martin Luther King was a sophomore at Morehouse at the time. That started that ball to rolling.

A lot of people said, "Buck, you were just born too soon." You were born—I said, "No, no, no, no, man I played with and against some of the greatest ballplayers ever lived." Had I been born earlier,

James "Cool Papa" Bell

I wouldn't have played against Babe Ruth. Mm-hmm. Yeah. I wouldn't have seen Cobb. Yes. I wouldn't have seen Rube Foster. I wouldn't have played against Oscar Charleston. I wouldn't have played against Josh Gibson or Satchel Paige. No, no. I was right on time.

With me, I wasn't thinking that way, as far as me having a chance of playing in the major leagues. No. I was past my prime. But, you know, what I wanted to do—now, I'm thinking about, Here's a chance for me to develop some young, black ballplayers to play Major League Baseball.

Well, I knew that was the death knell of Negro League baseball. See, this is something we had been hoping for all the time, because we thought if they integrated baseball, they were going to start integrating other things, see. And to tell you the truth, it hurt us in a way, because, see, I stayed at the Streets Hotel. The man that owned the Streets Hotel was black. The man that owned the bar in the Streets Hotel was black. The man that owned the restaurant in the Streets Hotel was black. The man that owned the barber shop in the Streets Hotel was black. So actually, see, when the Monarchs were in town, then people just coming from Omaha, Topeka, Wichita, all of these towns—St. Joe—coming here to baseball. So they spending a lot of money in the black neighborhood, see. After integration, we lost all of this.

What had most to do with it was this: When we played in Yankee Stadium for 40,000 people, Branch Rickey was playing over there in his ballpark, 20,000 people the same day. You understand? And 99⁹⁄₁₀ percent of those 40,000 we got in Yankee Stadium, black. That's a brand-new clientele. And Rickey was an astute businessman. He saw this. He saw this. And this is a capitalistic society. Money talks.

And well, one thing about it is, we wouldn't have had a chance with Landis, if he had been the commissioner at the time, see, but we got this guy, Happy Chandler. Now's the chance to move; Rickey saw a chance that he could do this now. And actually, I could understand the Yankees, Washington, the major league ballplayers not wanting to integrate for the simple reason was—actually, see, we played the Yanks—you know that 40,000 people we got at Yankee Stadium? That just didn't happen once; that happened often, you know, because all our teams were going into New York.

The Yankees got a percentage of using their ballpark, got all the concessions, not only there in Yankee Stadium, they had the franchise in Newark—the Newark (Negro League) ball club played in their ballpark. They got all the concessions, everything there. Kansas City, Yankee franchise, and this was our home field—they getting all the concessions here and getting everything. All of it. So it was money. The major leaguers was making money from Negro League baseball.

Well, in Havana, Cuba—I'm in Havana; I'm playing with Ha-

Jackie Robinson

vana. And Branch Rickey, you know, took the team to Havana for spring training because of the segregation in the South. And there was—that's when I met Jackie and his wife there. And see, we would go to see them in the morning, get their workout, and they would see us when we would play at night. And so, I was so happy that this had happened.

And let me tell you something about that Jackie Robinson. Jackie was different than we were, really. See, Jackie wasn't the best ballplayer we had in the Negro League, but he was the right guy, because, see—Hilton Smith told me this, because I was in the service when Jackie was—in 1945.

We'd been going to a filling station in Oklahoma for twenty years (with the Monarchs). We'd never gone to the restroom because the sign says, "White men only." Played that night in the town and next day, we go to the filling station and the man comes out. "Oh, you boys played a great game last night. You filled up the park. As usual, put on a great show." Put the hose in the tank. Jackie gets off the bus and starts toward the restroom. The man said, "Where you going, boy?"

"I'm going to the restroom."

"Boy, you know you can't go to that restroom."

Jackie said, "Take the hose out of the tank." Now, the man thought a little, see, because we got a fifty-gallon tank on this side, we got a fifty-gallon tank on that side. He ain't going to sell that much gas to one customer until we got back there again. You know what he said?

"You boys go to the restroom but don't stay long."

But the gist of that story is this: From that day on, the Monarchs never got gas at a station that they couldn't go to the restroom. They never played in a town that they didn't have a place for them to sleep or a place for them to eat. This is what Jackie did. See, we were acclimated to segregation, but not Jackie Robinson. That's what Jackie brought to us.

Yeah, went in the—this is what we started doing then, see, after that integration. Now, who it really hurt is the Willie Wells and Lenny Pearson. And these are ballplayers that could still play, but they're thirty years old in their prime. But the major leaguers didn't want these guys that old. See, Satchel went in because he was Satchel. Satchel went in because Bill Veeck knew he could draw.

Tom Greenway, scout for the Yankees, he came here and he's looking at Willie Brown and some of the older ballplayers that I had. And he said, "Buck, what do you think of these guys?"

I said, "They could play for you." I said, "But I got a guy—kid—standing in left field that you should look at." That was Elston Howard, yeah. He was in his early twenties.

I always wanted to be a manager by looking at Connie Mack. I saw Connie Mack with that straw hat looking good in the dugout. Mm-hmm. Then was Rube Foster in the dugout smoking that pipe, giving the signals, and things like that always—it fascinated me—

Ernie Banks

could be managing a ball club. And with the Monarchs, I was a captain there for years, just like running the ball club. And then when it was time for me to manage, it was a good time in my life and I really enjoyed it.

We always trained in a college—black college town. And we played the black college teams. So this was the black college—it was more or less like a minor league to us. And so I could evaluate the talent. We'd play against them and we'd see this kid. This kid can play. This kid can play. Not only for me—if I—if I—saw he could play and we didn't have any room for him, I would recommend him to the Memphis Red Sox or the Homestead Grays or somebody 'cause I wanted him to be playing.

In 1949, we got that—that little Monarch Team. We got them to playing and Cool Papa Bell is running this ball club for us. And they are playing all in the Northwest. And he saw a team from Texas playing. Then he saw this kid playing. And when he got here in Kansas City, their season was over, he got here.

He said, "Buck, I saw a guy playing on a team out of Dallas—he can play shortstop for you."

I said, "Yes. What's his name?"

"Ernie Banks."

So that fall I went down to Texas, to Dallas, and I signed Ernie. I had never seen him throw the ball but you know on Cool Papa's word. Then he played with us in 1950, went into service '51 and '52. Out of the service in '53 and now he's playing with us and oh man.

The guy went—and he just had it—he just had it. And this is when he comes to our East-West All-Star Game in Chicago and we are playing and the ball game was—our commissioner was Dr. Martin. They were just about to run out of balls and I got my bus there.

They said, "Buck, I'm just about to run out of balls. You better go out to your bus and get us—send out there and get us another dozen balls."

I said, "No, we've got them." We actually were trailing them by two runs. We got two men on base and Ernie Banks coming up to bat. I said, "Now, we don't need any more balls because this guy—this kid is going to end the ball game." Hit the ball in the left field stands and won the ball game.

And then that night, Tom Baird that owned the ball club, Tom called me and said, "Bring Banks out to Wrigley Field because they want to sign him to a Cub contract."

I said, "Okay." So he sent Wendell Smith, the writer. Wendell Smith came over and picked us up and took us out to Wrigley Field.

And that's when we signed him to that contract with the Cubs. But the guy that was the head of the scouting at the time, Wid Matthews, was the head of the scouting at Chicago. And he said— asked me—he said, "Buck now, this is—your baseball is just about over over there and Tom Baird is going to sell this ball club. When he sells it, I'd like for you to come and work for the Cubs as a scout." That sounded good to me. And he said, "Since you signed Ernie Banks to a contract with the Monarchs, I want you to sign him to this contract with the Cubs." So I signed Ernie Banks twice. And then yeah, that was in '53 and then I started working for the Cubs.

Horace Peterson was the head of the black archives here in Kansas City down at the 18th and Vine Street district. And he called me and he said, "Buck, come on. I want to talk to you."

I said okay. I got there.

He said, "Let's start a Negro League Hall of Fame."

I said, "Oh no, Horace, we don't need a Negro League Hall of Fame. I think the guys that's good enough should be in the Hall of Fame in Cooperstown."

So he said, "What would you suggest?"

I said, "Negro League Baseball Museum." So all right. This was in '90. So we got a little office. They wanted different things. They wanted the Jazz Hall of Fame and the Negro League Hall of Fame. That's what they wanted the money to do these things.

So that's when we started. They wanted me to take the Negro League Museum to Municipal Stadium. If you put it on that ground, you know all of the people coming—everybody can see it. I said, "No, no, no. The Negro Leagues Baseball Museum should be at 18th and Vine. This is where." So they tore all of that out and they—oh, we've got a beautiful place down there. And in the same building, it's the American Jazz Museum.

We've always had more good people than bad, but we just let the bad people do things that we shouldn't let them do. We are living in the greatest country in the world. And it's going to be greater. And your son, your grandson going to make it better. Mm-hmm. And it's your job to raise that boy. It's your job to raise that boy. You can admire an athlete or whatnot, but don't give him—that's not his job to raise your child.

DOM DIMAGGIO

Would Dom DiMaggio be a more recognizable figure today, or even a member of the National Baseball Hall of Fame, if his last name were Smith or if he had played for a team other than the Boston Red Sox? It has been said that he might have been the most underrated player of his time, and maybe of all time, because he labored under the enormous shadow of his brother Joe, as well as longtime teammate Ted Williams.

For many years Williams fought for his fellow outfielder to join him in the ranks of the immortals enshrined in Cooperstown. "Everything in life is comparison, and by every comparison I can make, Dominic stacks up awfully well," Williams said. "And that doesn't take into consideration things that aren't measured in black and white like fielding, spirit, and leadership." Dom's manager with the San Francisco Seals, Lefty O'Doul, warned him, "Everybody is going to compare you with your brother Joe. Every move you will make will be the basis for a comparison with what he does and how he does it. Don't forget that, but don't let it get you down. Just go ahead and do things your own way."

Though slight in stature and scholarly in appearance, the "Little Professor" compiled quite a résumé during his 11-year career. DiMaggio finished with 1,680 hits and a .298 batting average. But when you discount his three at-bat 1953 season, it was during his prime years, from 1940 to 1942 and from 1946 to 1952 (he was in the Navy from 1943 to 1945), that he excelled. In those ten seasons he had more hits (1,679) than anyone in the major leagues, only Williams scored more runs (1,144 to 1,046), and he was third in doubles behind Williams and Stan Musial.

Also a defensive stalwart, DiMaggio holds the American League career record for chances per game by an outfielder (2.99).

"He was as good a center fielder as I ever saw. Dom saved more runs as a center fielder than anybody else. Dom was a player who looked like a center fielder when he went back on a ball and an infielder when he came in for one. Only a great outfielder can do both, and that's what Dom was," Williams said. "And if the game was on the line and you needed a clean hit or a hard-hit ball, he was as good as anybody."

Joe Cronin, a Hall of Fame player, called him "one of the most perfect ballplayers I've ever seen. I believe he's actually the smartest young player I have watched in my time. Throws, runs, and thinks like a natural. I wouldn't ever hesitate to call him the best outfielder since I've been up."

DiMaggio's finest compliment may have come from Casey Stengel,

Dom DiMaggio

Joe DiMaggio's longtime manager with the New York Yankees, who once said, "With the possible exception of his brother Dom, Joe is the best outfielder in the league."

AS A BOY I was always very small in stature and they, both Joe and Vince, were ahead of me. So they played with the bigger guys and I sometimes was left out. But when we had the smaller guys playing, then of course I played. But as I got older then I started to play hardball along with softball. And we had a great playground in North Beach in San Francisco, and it's still a great playground there.

Dad thought it was a waste of time but Mother took it from the point of view that we were all young men and we liked to play games and this was a good game, nice and clean. Dad would find Vince's spikes and glove; he'd take them and throw them in the trash bin. And as fast as he did it, Mother would go out, take them out and hide them until the next time Vince was to use them. And he was the first one that this happened to. And he was the first one then to sign a professional baseball contract.

Vince was the first to get into the professional ranks. He went to Tucson, Arizona. And when he got back from Tucson, Arizona, you could have sopped him up with a blotter; he was so thin and lost so much weight. When Dad found out that he actually got paid for doing this, he said, "Well, that's a different story." When it became a matter of being paid for doing this, it changed everything. And when Joe got into the professional ranks, then we had Dad retire. From a point of throwing Vince's spikes and glove into the trash bin, after Joe made the breakthrough, Dad came to me and I was just a little guy at the time and said one day—I'll never forget—he said, "And when are you going to play baseball?"

With Joe, it was natural, it was just plain natural. From day one. He was an outstanding hitter with great power. In fact I think he was only about fourteen or fifteen years old. And on Sundays, once in a while, we'd go out to watch our older brother Tom play. And after they finished their first game, they were short one man in playing a game that the other team was to play but didn't show up. And so they had Joe play. And so, Joe went out and played and I think he came to bat and hit the ball—hit the ball pretty well.

He was very young. He broke in with his first year with San Francisco [the minor league San Francisco Seals of the Pacific Coast League]; he was only seventeen and immediately became a regular and started. That's when he had his fantastic season, first year in baseball.

I don't know how much [Seals Manager] Lefty O'Doul helped Joe. O'Doul had such a great talent and admiration for guys who had natural ability. For example, one day in San Diego I broke in with the Seals the year that Ted Williams was playing with San Diego. During batting practice, we're all sitting in our dugout watching batting practice, and Ted Williams is hitting for the San Diego Padres [of the Pacific Coast League] at the time. Lefty said, "I've got to go up and talk to this kid." So he runs out of our dugout and goes over to the third base side and waits for the kid to finish hitting.

When Ted got through Lefty went over and stopped him. And he said something to him. It couldn't have been more than twenty seconds, thirty seconds. Then he came back to the dugout. We all asked, "Lefty, what did you tell the kid?"

He said, "I told him very simply, 'Don't let anybody ever, ever fool with your batting stance and your hitting' " He says, "You are perfect."

Had it not been for Lefty, as far as hitting is concerned, I would never have made it to the majors—might not have made it in the minors. Yes. He made me, as I say, a batter that hit the ball with authority.

In all sincerity, my first ambition was—and this is factual—I wanted to play one year of professional baseball for my own satisfaction. Then when I got into it, things happened. The sports editor of the *San Francisco Daily News*, a fellow named Tom Laird, loved Joe and thought Joe was the greatest baseball player he had ever seen.

And he had a huge column and he would write, you know, praise Joe to the skies in his column and then he'd have paragraphs—and I don't know how to explain it, but then he would have a separate paragraph with italics. And he would refer to me as something that the San Francisco Seals were reflecting Joe's ability and they were using me because Joe was such a great player and it was going to be a help to them because of that. Well, that bothered me.

And I think that was when I became determined. I said, "Well, I'm going to do this and I'm going to get to the major leagues." This was all my own doing. And it wasn't too long. Right away they took me out of shortstop and put me in center field.

So one day at Seals Stadium I went way behind third base, picked up a ball and in the process of throwing it to first base it landed right up into the bleachers. And Mr. Charles Graham of the Seals said, "We have got to get that young man off that infield and put him in the outfield where we can use his arm." And that's how I ended up in center field.

We played at night and we played doubleheaders every Sunday. But we played the same team all week long. And we played doubleheaders on Sundays, and we traveled on Mondays. No games on Mondays. Rarely games on Mondays. Perhaps makeup. So that was the way the schedules were back then. We'd go to Sacramento, for example, in one week. We'd go to Seattle and Portland, which were fairly close together, and we'd play a week in Seattle and leave there and go to Portland and play a week in Portland.

Well, I could hit, but I would not have been able to hit in the professional ranks with my stance. I might have been a .200, .210, .215 hitter, and I would not have been hitting a lot of long balls. But the change that Lefty performed on me, that turned me completely from just a so-so hitter into a good hitter.

I learned this from Lefty O'Doul—one of the things I learned from Lefty—never guess. Anticipate, but never guess. He said, "Always look for the fastball, and you can always hit the fastball or the curveball off the fastball." That was the term we used, "You can hit the curveball off the fastball." So if you're looking for the fastball and the guy throws you a curve, even if you get fooled a little bit you can still hit it.

The Red Sox bought my contract from the Seals, and I signed a separate contract with them for my first year. My rookie salary might have been $7,500. I think it was $7,500, and the year I left and went into the Navy, it was $10,000.

When I went from the Seals to the Boston Red Sox in 1940 I was thrilled to death. I had complete inner confidence, not outwardly, but I had complete inner confidence that there was no question I would make it.

I had just hit .360 in the Pacific Coast League. I believe I lost the batting title by one point to Dom D'Alessandro. And I said, "They're going to be expecting great things, but I am going to just take it easy. I'm going to let line drives drop in front of me. I'm going to jog to first base. I'm not going to take big hard swings and try to hit the ball as far as I can—just keep my rhythm; hit line drives here, there, and everywhere, and just do that for a little while."

And that's exactly what I did, and there was a little concern. There was some little rumbling amongst the people and our clubhouse guy, John Orlando, came to me. He said, "Kid, you feeling all right?" He said, "You okay?"

I said, "I'm fine."

He said, "Are you all right? Are you sure you're all right?"

I said, "I am fine. I never felt better."

He said, "Well, okay. You know," he said, "people are wondering if, you know, if this is how you're playing."

I said, "No. Yes, I'm okay."

So then, when the first game—we played the first game against the Cincinnati Reds, an exhibition game. I said, "Well, now," I said, "I better play as good as I can." And I had quite a day, except I turned my ankle.

But it was obvious. I mean, I went out and caught balls and I scored. How I turned my ankle, there's an irony there. I was on second base and the bases were loaded and Johnny Peacock, our catcher, was on third base and the batter hit a line drive. My brother Vince was playing in right field for the Cincinnati Reds. And the batter hit a line drive to right field and I could see from where I was that the ball was going to fall in safely, so I took off for third base.

And Peacock jogged between going and not going, so I caught up to him, and there was only one out. I'm running right behind Johnny Peacock as we're coming into home plate. Well, the throw comes—Vince had a great arm—and I think Al Lakeman was the catcher at the time; and he reached out with his glove, and his toe was on home plate—he reached out to catch the ball and there was only one out; and Peacock, at the last minute, slides across home plate.

Well, I had just about started my slide when he slid, and if I had slid, my leg would have cut him up the back, so I turned my leg away from his body and it caught in the ground and that is how I sprained my ankle. The fact of the matter is, had Lakeman caught the ball, Peacock would have been out and I would have been safe.

It would've been one of the strangest plays ever heard of. But it didn't happen because Lakeman dropped the ball.

We got to Boston and I believe we had a doubleheader with the Philadelphia Athletics. It was early and for what reason, we had a doubleheader on Sundays, I guess. And it was wet and I came in for a low line drive and I skidded on the grass and the ball got away from me.

It bounced off and (Joe) Cronin then benched me. He said, "We're not going take a chance." I had just gotten over that bum ankle and when I slipped, we're not going to take a chance until the weather clears a little bit. So I was on the bench and Lou Finney took my place. Well, they couldn't get the guy out. Lou Finney was getting two, three, three, two [hits every game]; he was hitting like the best ever in his career.

So I was relegated to the dugout for quite a while. And I just assumed that I was going to be there for the rest of the year. But we were in Cleveland and Roger Cramer and Ted Williams collided on a ball, and I'll never forget, the ball landed safely. I think Ray Mack hit the ball and circled the bases. I think we lost the game 1-to-nothing, I believe. And Roger Cramer looked up and saw Teddy laid out on the field. And he went over—the ball was laying right there—Cramer got up and went over and laid down alongside Ted Williams and left the ball there.

They were both dazed and they had to help Teddy off the field. So Cronin—at that point, I didn't know where my glove was, and Cronin said, "DiMaggio," I said, "Who, me?" "Get out there and play left field." So I yelled and Johnny Orlando brought my glove down; I didn't even have my glove. And so I went out to left field.

And then when we got to Fenway Park, I played left field. And from Cleveland, we went back to Fenway Park; this was about the Fourth of July now, mind you. I had been on the bench all this time. And Lou Finney is still hitting like gangbusters, so I went out to left and performed quite well. And I remember Dick Bartell was playing for Detroit when we got back to Boston, and I'm playing left field. And he was a dead pull hitter, so I played him way over on the line and he hit the hardest line drive and I caught it in foul territory and he was fit to be tied.

"How can you catch a line drive in foul territory?" Well, anyhow, shortly after that, Cronin made the decision that I was going to play center field, and Cramer did not like that very much. He was very upset. Not that he had any animosity toward me, but he felt that he should be the center fielder. And the next year Roger was gone, but we always remained very close friends, Cramer and I.

Teddy was Teddy. We played the first year, 1937, in the Pacific Coast League, together. He was with San Diego, I was with San Francisco. And he went up during the '38 season, but for whatever reason, he was sent to Minneapolis. And finished the '38 season in Minneapolis. So he played one year with the Red Sox, in 1939, and then I came up and joined the club in 1940. But there was never any animosity between Teddy and me, or any ill feelings; we got along very nicely. As a matter of fact, I'd like to just interject this: When I reported to Sarasota in spring training, I met everyone on the ball club. And Jimmie Foxx was one of the last ones to come in. He came over to my locker, welcomed me, patted me on the back, and he said, "Welcome kid." He says, "Good luck."

Lefty Grove

And then one thing and another and he went over to his locker. Lefty Grove came in, walked past me, went to his locker, said nothing; I realized it, I said nothing; I didn't know who Grove was. For two weeks—two solid weeks—we even rode up and down the elevator in the morning and sometimes in the evening; he never spoke to me and I never spoke to him.

And one day a friend of mine—well not a friend of mine, but he became a very close friend of mine, Jimmy Foready, was in the hospital and they didn't know whether he was going to make it or not. And Wes Palmer, from Rochester, Maine, wherever he was, asked if I would go out to visit Jim Foready. He had been asking for me and so, sure, I went out. On the way, Mr. Palmer said, "I understand you don't talk to Lefty Grove."

I said, "Mr. Palmer, you have it wrong."

He said, "What you mean?"

I said, "Lefty Grove does not speak to me."

He said, "Well," he says, "don't you think you ought to go up and say hello to Lefty Grove?"

I said, "No." I said, "That's the incorrect thing for me to do." I said, "I think it's up to Mr. Grove to come to me and say hello to me."

He said, "Well." He said, "Why don't you just forget it." He said, "You know, Grove is a strange kind of a guy."

I said, "Well, I just feel funny about doing it." I said, "I'm not one who idolizes people." I said, "I like them, I admire them." I said, "But I just don't feel it's my position." Well we got to the hotel in Sarasota, the Terrace Hotel, and there are wrought iron rocking chairs all lined up on the terrace and there's a screen door.

And who's sitting by the screen door as I entered? To the left, in the first seat, is Lefty Grove, and Johnny Orlando, our clubhouse boy, is sitting in the second seat, on these wrought iron rockers. So I went to open the screen door. I was going to go into the lobby, and I said, "Oh, well." I said, "What the heck." So I turned and I said, "Hello, Lefty." And I stuck my hand out.

With this, Grove jumped out of his chair, hugged me, grabbed Johnny Orlando, our clubhouse boy—he was strong—grabbed our clubhouse boy and lifted his body and said, "Let Dommie sit here."

So I sat down and we must have talked for fifteen, twenty minutes. It couldn't have been a more gracious welcome. It was just great and we became very, very close friends. Very close friends. I played an All-Star Game in Philadelphia after Lefty retired, and I was sitting in the clubhouse and somebody came along and we had just those singular lockers—and somebody came along and whacked me across the shoulder, knocked me into the locker, and I said, "Lefty Grove, you so-and-so!" I turned around and, sure enough, it was Lefty Grove.

Well, Lefty Grove was a big guy and I had known about the prowess in his younger day when he would just throw fastballs by people, when he was with the Athletics. But when I got up to the

Red Sox, Lefty had seen his greatest days, his best days, and was actually striving to gain his 300th victory. That he wanted more than anything, and he was having a hard time doing it. So I really didn't see Lefty Grove in his heyday.

At one point in Washington, Lefty had pitched a fabulous ball game. He'd lost 2-to-1 or 2-to-nothing, something like that, and I'm sitting next to him. He was on the edge of the bench in the clubhouse and I was next to him, and I had started to take my uniform off and we sat there for the longest time. Nobody said a word. He didn't say anything. I didn't say anything. And finally, I said, "Gee, I've got to break this up." So I turned to him and I said, "Lefty," I said, "boy, that was a tough one to lose." I said, "You should have won it."

With that, he took his shirt—he hadn't even unbuttoned it—he took his shirt and spread the bottom shirts one to the right and one to the left and the buttons popped right off his chest. And he turned to me and he said, "If they had all played like you did, we would have won in nine." I'll never forget that.

He had a habit of going off for two or three days, and he had, I think it was twenty-five-year-old Black Label, whatever it was. He always had it in his locker. He was the only person who was allowed to have this privilege. But he would go off and not report for two or three days and just stay away because something that didn't set well with him happened, and then he'd come in as if nothing happened and nobody paid attention to it. He was a very colorful guy. He didn't have the gift of gab, far from it, but he was just a nice guy and a gruff guy.

Ted Williams, for example, had a habit of waiting for me if I was on base. Of course, he couldn't talk to me, but if, for one reason or another, I was out, then he'd wait for me to return to the dugout and he knew what the guy had.

And he said, "Well, Dommie, is he fast today? What does he got?"

And I always answered him. I'd say, "He doesn't look this or he does this."

Ted Williams

And one day I did not hit a ball that I felt I should have hit and as I'm coming into the dugout, he said something about, "Dommie, what's he got?"

I says, "I don't know."

And he turned to me and he said, "Well, what kind of a dumb hitter are you? You don't even know what the guy's throwing you." And I laughed. That was the end of that.

I'll tell you, when I got into Yankee Stadium, the adrenaline flowed. I just loved playing in Yankee Stadium. I had all that room out there in center field and I was a line drive hitter. I enjoyed Yankee Stadium very much. I made a few great catches there. I made a couple on Charlie Keller—one day, two of them—that brought me out by the monuments in center field and I thought they were going to shred—pick me up in pieces. I didn't dare take my eye off the ball and I should have, but I just—I went pretty close to those monuments on two of those occasions. I loved playing against New York, and when they came to Boston, you could cut the atmosphere with a knife. It was just so full of tension. I mean just great.

Jimmie Foxx was the nicest guy you'd ever want to meet. He was such a gentleman, just an easygoing guy. I guess he must have been five-ten or so. Very strong. I actually saw Jimmie start to swing at a ball, and it was down low, and he stopped it, just about the time the ball was horizontal with the ground, and his feet went out from under him and he landed prone, on his entire right side. I said, "Now, that's strength!" He just stopped the bat and his body went out from under him. Very strong.

We had an exhibition game against the Cincinnati Reds.

And I was on second base and he had 3-and-2, and as the pitch came, I started for third and he hit a ball. I stopped in my tracks and I turned around to look. Back then they had a huge laundry sign, way behind the left field fence. And I looked and that ball hit the top of the laundry sign and disappeared. I couldn't believe a ball could be hit that far. But he had great power. He also caught, you know; he was a first baseman.

Oh, we'd go out to dinner and I'd leave him at a quarter to twelve; we had a twelve o'clock curfew and I'd leave him at a quarter to twelve at night. He'd stay there and he'd invite people from the next table to come over. And the funny part of it was he'd end up picking up the tab. He was that kind of a guy.

I just didn't [drink]. We'd have a couple of beers, you know— two, maybe three on occasion—but that was it. We'd stay in the clubhouse. I made it a rule never to take the game home with me. I left it in the clubhouse. After I was married, I always left it in the clubhouse. And I would stay there maybe an hour or an hour and a half, after the game, and have a couple of beers before I dressed to leave. Maybe something happened at a game, because I took it very seriously and I loved the game and I hated to see mistakes and dumb plays and people not—not that they did back then—everybody hustled and played the game 100 percent, but rarely—I don't remember anybody just plain laying down; they wouldn't be there, because we had somebody looking over our shoulder all the time. So I just had no desire to drink more than a couple of beers and so that was that.

I did smoke during those years. I don't think I ever smoked more than a package of cigarettes a day. And it was funny, we'd come in after each inning, and everyone would go down into the runway and they had cigarettes; they had water pipes around the dugout underneath the steps. And everybody had their own cigarette scattered somewhere along the place, and everybody knew where their cigarette was. So they would take a couple of puffs, put it out, and put it back where it was.

I often wondered how I would react to facing Bob Feller. I took a couple of pitches and I finally settled down and was a little tense at first, but I settled down. To the best of my knowledge, Bobby never, ever purposely threw at anybody. I don't think he even tried to brush anybody back. He just had enough stuff that he didn't have to do that. Now everybody talks about how fast he threw, and he threw fast and he threw hard. Very seldom do you hear anybody mention his curveball.

Just picture standing at home plate and here's a guy throwing 105, 106 miles an hour and then he a starts a curveball at your eyes and when it gets through breaking, it's down in your ankles. If you stop to think of that, you don't have very much time to decide what the pitch is going to do, so you've got to prepare to make sure it's not that fast. Well, you're looking for that fastball. Like Lefty O'Doul said, "Oh, you look for the fastball. Hit the curve off the fastball."

So you're always looking for the fastball, and if he starts it up there, you say, "Well, it's either—I'm either going to have to duck or it's going to curve," and you've got to be ready for it. So you have to have the agility of trying to get—be prepared to get your head out of the way, yet have your body get in there so that if the ball breaks, you can take a swing at it or take a little cut at the ball.

(Red) Ruffing and (Spud) Chandler had the rising fastballs, you know. If they had been pitching in the last few years in the major leagues and they were calling strikes below the belt, guys like Ruffing and (Vic) Raschi wouldn't have lasted because they threw up around your letters all the time—letters and shoulder high. If you swung at a letter fastball, the next one would be about two inches higher, and if you swing at that, the next one would be two inches higher. They had great control, but they had rising fastballs, and they never threw around the belt. Everything was above the belt.

In '41: Lefty Grove won his 300th victory. Ted Williams hit the famous home run in the All-Star Game; and I was kneeling in the circle. I was in the on-deck circle. There were two out, two men on, and Teddy was at bat, and they had a big powwow out on the mound, and I, to this day, I don't know what they were talking about.

I said, "They're not thinking about pitching to him." I said, "They will put him on and pitch to me." Claude Passeau was the pitcher, but I believe that Passeau had struck Williams out the time before, so they decided to pitch to Ted and Ted hit the barrier in right field, against the wall, and we won the ball game. And then in the World Series, that was the year that Mickey Owen lost the pitch and hot Tommy Henrich got to first base on the strikeout.

And, of course, the war was declared after the season ended in December, and the changes started after the '41 season. We never had air-conditioning when we played. Always traveled by train. There was limited television in the big leagues, and when the war was over—by the time the war was over, we stayed in hotels with air-conditioned rooms. We started to fly by plane. Shortly after '46, Jackie Robinson broke the black barrier. So things happened. Johnny Murphy started to try to get pensions for the players. He was railroaded. After he was railroaded, Freddy Hutchinson took up the slack, and in order to get Freddy—well, they didn't make him manager of the Detroit ball club to get rid of him, but having

Joe DiMaggio

become the manager, he had to give up his effort on the players' behalf, and all of those things did happen. And it was a great, great year—good, bad.

Of course we were watching Ted hit .400 in '41, and there was my brother Joe's hitting streak. We were aware of Joe's streak. The evidence was there. Yeah, we played against him and playing at Fenway Park, we had the scoreboard in left field, and Teddy always talked to the scoreboard keeper and would get the news—how's Joe doing—and every time Joe got a hit, "Dommie, Dommie," he would call over to me, and he'd say, "Joe got a base hit in the second inning, third inning, first," all that stuff, and he'd keep me posted. So that's how I knew. When we were playing at Fenway, I got the answers right away when Joe got a base hit.

One recollection of playing against him during the streak sticks out in my mind. I made quite a long speech about it at the ALS banquet one night. Joe was out on the first trip and then a second trip. He hit a shot to left center field that—so many things ran through my mind, and the bases were loaded, I believe, at the time, and he was fighting for the runs batted in title. And I went out and I caught this ball in the tip of my web and as soon as I caught it, I got a sick feeling to my stomach. I said, "Oh, my God." You know, this is his third time at bat. The next time at bat, he hit the ball into the seats so that nobody could catch it.

On the way in, after I caught the ball—and this was the third out of the inning—he was coming out to his place in center field and I'm—I've got to pass this guy, and, gee, and I'm feeling so sorry and then I turn to give him an apologetic look and he looked—he just turned at the same time and he looked at me—believe me, if

Enos Slaughter

looks could kill, I would have dropped right there, and I said, "Oh, my God. I made an enemy."

During the 1942 season, I enlisted in the Navy. I went down to the Federal Building in Boston during midseason and I enlisted.

An acquaintance of mine, a fellow named Chase, was talking to me about it and I said, "I wouldn't mind enlisting in the Navy." I said, "I'll go down."

We went downtown and when I was given the test, the eye test, I recall the doctor saying, "Well, read the chart as far down as you can."

And I said to him jokingly, I said, "What chart?"

He had me take my glasses off. He said, "Can't you see the chart?"

I said, "Well, I think I can make the big E out. I can't see much of anything else."

He said, "Well, why don't you walk up to the wall," and being, at that time, I guess I was a little funny, I just walked into the wall and then he laughed and I laughed and backed up. And he said, "Dom, the Navy's not going to accept you. Why? Because your eyesight is a detraction. They just won't accept you."

I said, "But I've been wearing glasses," and that's what they don't want. You know, they want somebody—you're going to be in the Navy, you're going to be in the service, you have to be able to see without your glasses. And I said, "Well, isn't there anyplace?" No. So it was pretty a much a no, and we talked for the longest time. You know, he had guys waiting outside. And I said, "Well, doc," I says, "what would happen if I try to get into the Army? Would the Army take me? Would the Army draft me?"

He said, "The chances are forty percent they might take you."

I said, "Well, why can't the Navy take me if the Army's going to?" I says, "I'd rather be in the Navy."

Well, to make a long story short, after the longest time, he said, "There is one possibility and this is it. I could draft a letter to the War Department recommending that because of your athletic ability, it offsets your eyesight," this, that, and the other, "and have the staff here at the Federal Building, the entire staff, sign a letter and send it to the War Department in Washington. Would you like me to do that?"

I said, "By all means." Sixty days later, I got the notice that I had been accepted in the Navy, but they weren't going to call me until sometime in October or November, which meant that I could finish the season. So I finished the '42 season.

For the record, I'd like to say and state that, not only do I believe I was the first ever to break in as a professional, but I broke in from the sandlots into Triple A wearing glasses and then came to the major leagues. Even after I got to the major leagues on my own statistics, they still referred to me as a question mark and whether I was there because of Joe and Joe's reputation. But when I finally made the breakthrough—about halfway through the second year I was up and I made a big breakthrough—then the floodgates opened up. And kids with glasses played athletics everywhere. And the pros brought them up.

We had a pretty good team in 1946 and we beat the Yankees for the one and only time. If we had a real good catcher and a little pitching, we would have won our share of pennants, but we didn't.

The big thing that sticks out in my mind is what affected me personally and affected, probably affected, the World Series. That was when Slaughter made his famous run around the bases. Harry "the Hat" Walker was the batter, and a notorious left field hitter. In the top half of the eighth inning, we were behind 3-to-1. And we got the first two guys, I think Catfish Metkovich singled, Rip Russell doubled, so we had men on third and second and nobody out. So the Cardinals replaced Murry Dickson with the left-hander—Harry Brecheen. Brecheen came in to pitch because we had Wally Moses, left-handed hitter leading off, and Johnny Pesky, left-handed hitter, hitting second. I was hitting third that year. So he got both of those guys out. And I'm the next batter. They had a little powwow. I had a pretty good success, Brecheen and me, in intrasquad games we used to play. And he had pretty good luck against Ted.

So they were talking and I said, well, what are these guys talking about. The only thing I could think it was, well, don't feed him anything too good. You know, give him a lot of stuff and see if he'll go after a bad ball. Well, I figured pretty much that out. And then I got him—I worked him down to a 3-and-1 count. I looked down at Cronin and Cronin had the hit sign on all the way. So now I keep my foot out of the box and I'm thinking and I'm thinking and I'm thinking. I'm thinking to myself, they want me to swing at a pitch.

I said if he throws me a curveball, he can't get it over—Brecheen could never get his curveball over. I said he's not going to throw me a curveball because he can't get it over and I'm going to walk. And then Teddy comes up with the bases loaded. He's not going to throw me a fastball because if he hit me between the eyes, he wouldn't hurt me with his fastball. So the only pitch he can throw me is a screwball and he's not going to throw it inside so I could pull it. He's going to throw it to try to hit the outside corner. I had figured that out in that short period of time. It takes longer to tell.

So I stepped back in the box and I am saying with 3-and-1, I am going to look for the screwball, which I rarely have but in this instance, it was natural. Sure enough here comes a screwball as big as a balloon, just a little bit heading for the outside corner. I said if he does that—throws that pitch, he thinks I'm going to try to pull the ball. I'm going with it. So I swung and hit the ball to right center field. And when it hit, went off the bat, I thought it was a line drive going to be between the two outfielders. So I'm thinking to myself, I'm going to try to get to third base, because if I get to third base and they're pitching to Teddy, I have to be very careful because I have pride in myself on being able to get into the home plate. On any fastball, I would have scored.

So in the process that I'm turning first base, I dig for a little extra and I pull a muscle in my leg. And I barely get to second base. Later—(Enos) Slaughter told me, he said, Dom, he said, if the ball would have been another foot and a half toward center field, it would have landed in the seats because they had a screen. You know they had the wall and then they had a screen on top of the wall. Another foot and a half toward center field would have been in the seats. I didn't realize that. Evidently, the ball had taken off. I thought it was going to be a line drive between the two fielders.

So we held up the game a long time. Finally I had to leave because Joe Cronin said, "Dom," he said, "I'll tell you, if Ted gets a base hit," he says, "you can't score on this. And you might have caused permanent damage." Well I really didn't want to leave but I—I realized I had to. And so I had to leave. And in the bottom of the eighth, up comes Harry Walker with Slaughter on first base and two out. And we're trying to move Leon Culberson over.

I was out at the dugout. I was trying to get Culby to move over. Culberson is playing center field. Now, Harry Walker hits his patented line drive over the shortstop's head. And it's going between Ted and Culberson. So now Culberson has to backtrack to make sure the ball doesn't get by the two of them so he backtracks. And I said ever since it happened, I said I would never have had to backtrack. I would have been over enough that I would have made a right-angle turn and cut the ball off.

And I said all along that I would have had a shot at Slaughter at third base. I'd already thrown three guys out in that series and they had stopped running. They had stopped running. And so that's the first thing Slaughter said after the game was over. He said, when I got to third base, I realized they had taken DiMaggio out of the game. And then he decided to go on in.

In 1948, somebody came up to me. I don't recall who it was even, came up to me and says, "Dom, you have just been elected the American League player representative."

I said, "On what basis?" Never found out who or why. Never. I have to assume that all the players voted, because I didn't know anything about my own Red Sox team. But I was told I had been elected the American League player representative. And I said, "Well, okay. Fine." I already was the Red Sox player representative.

My role was to meet with the executives in baseball and talk about player concerns. Marty Marion was elected the National League player representative. He was the Cardinal shortstop. We were the player representatives. And the baseball executive committee arranged a meeting for us to air whatever gripes or complaints we might have.

It was an effort that I saw Johnny Murphy put in, I saw Fred Hutchinson put in. I saw no reason why, at this point, why shouldn't I? If they wanted me, I was already the Red Sox player representative. If they felt I should be the guy, then, by all means, I was going to do it. And so when we were advised that there would be a meeting that we would air our differences, I got in touch with Marty Marion.

I said, "Marty," I said, "we've got to get together." I said, "I will draw up a list of complaints and gripes amongst our players, and you do it with your players." And I said, "And then, we've got to compare these lists." I said, "Because it would be foolish for you and me to appear between these guys, and you air the same complaints I do or vice versa." So I said, "Let's go over the list." And we eliminated a lot of duplication, so that when he had his say and I had my say, there was no duplication whatsoever. We talked about conditions on the field. Probably meal money and that sort of thing. And a pension. We felt that a pension was very much desired.

After we aired our business, I recall, very distinctly, they said, "Well, we've accepted your complaints. We'll give them some thought. But, in turn, we would like to make a suggestion."

Of course, Marty and I said, "Yeah, well, what's that?"

They said, "We'd like for your players to conduct themselves in a more gentlemanly manner, by proper dress at restaurants and in lobbies."

No problem. We said, "That certainly will be done." And then I said, "As long as we're bringing up certain things," I said, "there is a practice currently going on that can boomerang against baseball." And I said, "It's a dangerous practice. And it should be stopped, because it could be a bombshell where baseball is concerned."

And they said, "What's that?"

I said, "There is peeking through scoreboards and signs are being given to coaches and passed on to the batters." I said, "And it's something that has got to be stopped."

Walter O'Malley (of the Dodgers) jumped out of his seat and said, in no uncertain terms, he said, "You are absolutely right." He said, "I will pass word amongst my entire organization first thing tomorrow morning to put a stop to it."

Well, he shocked me. He shocked me. Because, here I thought Cleveland was the only team. Well, it kind of stunned me and took me aback. But then, I recovered, and I said, "Yes, Mr. O'Malley."

And I said, "There is, at least, one other guilty party in this group," because Oscar Vitt of the Indians, who was there, knew his team had been doing it.

From my personal point of view, I was extremely curious to see how I, actually, would compare with a black center fielder. To see whether there would be any significant difference. And of course, Luke Easter, also, came in very shortly after that.

In all honesty and sincerity, I don't recall our ball club yelling racial slurs at black players. You know, they would have guys on the dugout steps, I was told, yelling slurring remarks at these people. But I don't recall that happening.

These guys all became pretty outstanding ballplayers, and the Red Sox still didn't have any, I think, then, the players started to think, well, hey, listen. You ought to get some of these black players up here, because they're pretty good ballplayers. I mean, we might have thought that.

We were in an exhibition game in Brooklyn, against the Dodgers. Cal Hubbard, who I had a great deal of admiration for, was an umpire and one of the best. I was sliding into second base when Jackie Robinson made a swish at me with the ball. And when I slid, my uniform blew out, and Hubbard called me safe. And Jackie Robinson ran up to Cal, and he said, "I tagged him. I tagged him."

And Cal Hubbard said, "I didn't see it that way."

So he didn't carry on too long. But Jackie Robinson, then, left and started to go back to his position. And Cal Hubbard came over to kick second base, on the premise that he was kicking second base.

And as an aside, without turning his head, he said, "Dom, did he touch you?"

In the same way, I turned toward center field, and I said, "Cal, I felt something brush the back part of my shirt." I said, "I think it was his glove."

He said, "Okay. Thanks." He was testing to see, you know, what the reaction was. He said, "Thank you." And that was the end of it.

On the Yankees Bill Dickey was one ballplayer I admired. And I'll tell you, Keller, Henrich, great guys. Rizzuto was a real enigma. God, he'd get into the hole and, no sooner he had the ball, it was on its way to first. He didn't have a strong arm. But for some reason, he got it away faster than anybody. He'd just get you by that half a step. Oh, there were other guys that I admired.

Red Rolfe was at third base. Dickey, I admired even before the war. He was, I believe, a lieutenant commander. And we had a World Series in the Pacific area. And I was in Australia with Phil Rizzuto and a few other players. And the saying goes that [Admiral Chester] Nimitz and [General Douglas] MacArthur bet a case of liquor. Now, they had all the best players on the Hawaiian islands at the time, were in the Army. So MacArthur, supposedly, challenged Nimitz to a World Series in the Hawaiian islands. And Nimitz, who had bet, supposedly, a case of liquor, said, "Fine." So he went back to his office, and he got his secretary. And said, "Where are all of our best Navy players?"

And the guy said, "Well, there's some in the Great Lakes." They had Johnny Mize, Johnny Vander Meer, Schoolboy Rowe. And he said, "We've got a couple, Mr. Feller is on the *Alabama*. And we've got a couple in Australia. DiMaggio and Rizzuto and Padgett."

And he (Nimitz) said, "Bring them in."

"Well, yes, sir. I'll get the paperwork done as soon as I can."

He said, "How long will it take you?"

He said, "Probably, a day and a half, two days. I'll get the paperwork done."

And he said, "You bring the players in, and we'll take care of the paperwork later."

"Yes, sir."

So they brought in guys from the Great Lakes and brought Phil Rizzuto and me in from Australia.

We slaughtered the Army. We slaughtered them.

As far as baseball goes, it's a clean-cut game. Everything is right there before you. You see everything. And the integrity of the game had been unblemished and outstanding during our days. I'm not overly pleased about what has happened in recent years, with the labor strikes and strikes which should never have happened. The fans took what happened previously. But I don't think they'll take another one. And I believe management and employees should be able to get together and iron this thing out. The game was a national pastime for all those many years, and those of us who played it years ago, played really, specifically, first, for the love of the game.

Money came later, because we had no choice, really. Because we were, sort of, peasants. I mean, slaves, because we had no choice. But we would negotiate and do the best we could, as far as money was concerned. And then, we'd go out and play our hearts out. It has, now, since been opened to everyone. It was limited to just the Caucasians, the whites. The blacks have made their breakthrough.

Now, it's expanded internationally. We always had a few Canadian players. But now, we have Japanese and we have South Americans and it's branched out. I think it's just a wonderful, wonderful game. And I hope they don't do anything to hurt it.

There is—you know Vince is an excellent example of the difference between our players during our time and today's players. Vince batted .245, .250 and hit 20, 25 home runs. Excellent outfielder—great. It was a toss-up as to whoever is better—was the better outfielder between Joe, Vince, and myself. And it was hard for him to hook on with a major league team as a regular for any length of time.

And he got peanuts for playing. Today he, with his statistics, would be three or four million dollars a year. And that's the difference. I think it's watered down because of the expansion over the leagues. And I think it's wonderful that three of us, the last three born of nine children, ended up playing professional baseball and going on from there.

I enjoyed my entire baseball career. I was fortunate to have a manager (Lefty O'Doul) in the minor leagues who could give me the requisites I required. I enjoyed coming to the major leagues, playing with the Red Sox. I enjoyed taking the responsibility of being a first player representative. My most satisfying part of baseball I believe is making the breakthrough, wearing glasses, coming off of sandlots into AAA baseball, and then on to the majors.

I don't believe that ever happened before. And once I made the breakthrough in the majors, it opened the gates for all of those young people who wore glasses and were always discriminated against because they could not wear the glasses and play professional sports. As far as my efforts in life, I wouldn't have changed my career for anything.

I enjoyed a challenge and I think my whole history points to the fact that I faced these challenges and accepted them and they became a good part of my life.

JOHNNY PESKY

According to the dictionary, pesky *is defined as "causing annoyance" or "troublesome." Though he was born John Michael Paveskovich, a name change to Johnny Pesky seemed apropos considering all he brought to a baseball field.*

A sure-handed infielder and magician with a bat, Pesky was a star shortstop when he came up with the Boston Red Sox in 1942, batting .331, scoring 105 runs, and finishing third in the American League MVP race. After spending three years in the service, Pesky came back in 1946, batting .335, scoring 115 runs, and finishing fourth in the MVP voting. In fact, over his first seven big league seasons he would average .315 and 109 runs scored.

One anonymous veteran American League pitcher, assessing Pesky's skills, said, "That Pesky is a tough little monkey to pitch to. You see, we pitchers figure that hitters of the caliber of Ted Williams, Joe DiMaggio, and Hank Greenberg are going to get their share of hits no matter how we pitch to them. They get good wood on the ball most of the time and some of their line drives are going to land in there safe. So we concentrate on keeping the men ahead of them in the batting order off the bases. That's why pitching to a little pest like Pesky is real tough in a close game. He's always on those bags, even though we bear down on him. And then up comes Williams with that long ball and we're behind."

Though he may be best remembered for a play in the seventh game of the 1946 World Series, where the Cardinals's Enos Slaughter scored the winning run from first base when Pesky is thought to have hesitated in his relay throw home—something that Pesky vigorously disputes, as you'll see—no one should forget what a fine career he had. In his ten seasons, mostly spent with the Red Sox, he finished with 1,455 hits, leading the league three times, and a .307 batting average.

Pesky's one-time manager in Boston, Joe Cronin, once compared him to some of the game's all-time greats. "The way he handles that bat, you have to call him a modern model of Ty Cobb or a Willie Keller. John drags, bunts, hits the ball into the ground and scampers down the line, and pokes to all fields. He can even pull a long ball when it means something. But what makes him especially valuable to a team's offense is his speed. He can fly around the bases."

Hall of Fame pitcher Ted Lyons remarked, "The real spark of that club is Johnny Pesky. Ted Williams and Rudy York pace the power. But

Johnny Pesky

Pesky is the pivot of the defense, and he keeps the opposition infield in a turmoil. He bunts and drags and punches and drives."

Still a fixture in the game, Pesky has spent more than fifty years with the Red Sox as a player, coach, manager, radio and television announcer, and advertising salesman. Pesky understands the travails the game brings. "Baseball can build you up to the sky one day," he said, "and the next day you have to climb a stepladder to look up to a snake."

I GRADUATED HIGH SCHOOL and I signed that August with the Red Sox and I've been with them sixty years.

I had a glove in my hand all the time, even in the wintertime, except when we went to the ice rink. And my father would say, you'll be a baseball player, John. You're going to be a bum. He didn't know anything about baseball and he never—he saw me play one game as a semipro. And he didn't know anything about baseball. He knew boccie but he didn't know baseball.

I had a few years being a clubhouse boy in the Pacific Coast League. Those years in the Coast League, that's where I saw Joe DiMaggio. I saw his brother Vince, Bobby Doerr, Ted Williams. I was a clubhouse boy in '35 and '36.

Eddie Collins was the general manager with the Red Sox—now this was in '36 or '37. I think this was '37, 1937, and Eddie Collins, the old second baseman, Hall of Famer, and a wonderful man and he came out to watch. He had talked Mr. (Tom) Yawkey into buying the ball club [San Diego Padres]. Well, anyway, he was looking for some players. He wanted to get some youth in there. So he comes out to the Coast League and he's going to stay about four or five days to watch George Meyer, who was playing shortstop. And Bobby Doerr was playing second base, and he had Williams in left field. So Collins is there. He's watching them.

And he was going to leave after about four or five days, but he decided to stay two or three extra days. Now, it came time, the owner of the San Diego club was a man by the name of Bill Star.

Eddie Collins

And he and Eddie Collins must have been close friends. So Star said to Collins, he says, "How about the shortstop and second baseman?"

And Collins told him, he says, "I don't want the shortstop. I want the second baseman and the left fielder."

And Star, these were his exact words because I heard this, but he says, it has to be true. He told Collins, he says, "You don't want that guy in left field, he's nuts." You know, he was a cantankerous guy and Williams was unusual, one of the brightest guys as we got to go, you know, to play together and all this sort of thing. And I can, I can still see him. He's standing in the outfield before the pitcher is warming up; he's out there practicing his swing; and he was, he was really something. And he had a great swing and Lefty

O'Doul told him, he says, "Ted, don't let anybody change your swing."

They had put me on the major league roster. And Eddie Pellagrini was the other kid, he was out at San Diego. And when I got to spring training I didn't know what was going to happen. But Joe Cronin was pretty good. He was good with Pelly and I; he'd play me one day and he'd play Pelly the next day. And Pelly was a little guy, he wasn't as big as I was, and he was trying to hit the ball out of the ballpark. We used to talk, I said, a great kid; we're great friends to this day. I says, "Pelly, use what you've got. You're not six-two and 195 pounds. You're going to just, you're going to hit balls right, the best 325-foot fly ball you ever saw." But he wanted to rip that ball, and I says, "Use what you've got. If you hit a ball on the ground, run like a scalded dog and you can beat out a base hit and stuff like that. Bunt and drag and do these sort of things."

But he wouldn't do it, he was just—out in that spring, Joe would play Eddie, he'd play me, he'd play Eddie, he'd play me, but then Eddie come up about two weeks into spring training and he come up lame or something.

And I had to go over to St. Pete, play against the Cardinals and the Yankees. And so I had two pretty good days against them. I remember throwing DiMaggio out; I backhanded a ball and I was playing it way over in the hole and he hit a rocket and I backhanded the ball and threw him out. I mean, it was hit so hard I couldn't help, I could have bounced the ball over there and got him out. Well, anyway, Cronin went along with this. So finally it came down where he had to cut to twenty-five players.

And he hasn't said a word to either Pelly or me. So I said, oh boy. So I was playing pretty well and there was nothing wrong with me physically. And I'd have gone out there on a broken leg if I had to, just to play. Well anyway, we're getting ready to leave. He calls in Pelly and he sends him to Louisville. And he didn't say a word to me. So now, we break camp in about four or five days. We're going up to Atlanta and Birmingham. Now, we're in Kentucky. We'd play all the way north to Boston.

We played Cincinnati. And Cronin hadn't said a word to me,

but we had Skeeter Newsome, who was a veteran player and a wonderful little guy. And Cronin hadn't said a word, so we're playing Cincinnati. We're in—I'll never forget that we played them in Atlanta. We played them at Birmingham. We were playing up in Kentucky someplace, I should remember the name. It was a great horse area. Well, anyway, we were playing and Vander Meer is pitching.

And it was a beautiful spring morning, spring day, and we're doing, about the fifth inning, I hit a ball to right center field off of Vander Meer. And I got a triple out of it, so we score a couple of runs and Cronin comes over to me after the inning, and he says, "Kid, you just made the ball club." That's how that happened. I thought sure he was going to send me to Louisville, but he didn't.

Spud Chandler was a 20-game winner for the Yankees. In '41 I think he won 20 games. And he was tough. He threw a hard sinker and we were playing a game in August in Boston and for some reason Jack Malaney was in our dugout before the game and Chandler's to pitch. He's going through his book and he, and I was there and Malaney and me and Ted was sitting maybe from here to the table over there.

And Malaney said, "Johnny, you don't have a hit off of this guy." He goes through the book, 0-for-4, 0-for-3, 0-for-3, 0-for-4. I was 0-for-14 off of him.

And Williams hears this and here he comes. He says, "For crying out loud," he says, "I'm a foot taller, forty pounds heavier, and I can't pull him." He says, "You're trying to pull this guy, what are you trying to do?" He said, "That isn't your stroke anyway." And he's just chewing me out. And I'm going, yeah, I'm just looking at him.

So the game starts. The first two times up I'm pulling him. Two groundballs to Gordon, two outs. So I'm now in the bottom of the eighth inning, we have two outs and our big catcher is— (Bill) Conroy's on first base. Dominic (DiMaggio) hits a ball down the right field line that Henrich gets back. Now, the guy on first base, Conroy, cannot score from first. Now, I'm the next hitter with two outs.

So Bill Dickey goes out to talk to Chandler. In the meantime Ted grabs me by the sleeve and he says, "Now, Johnny, listen to me. Don't try to pull this guy." He says, "For God sakes, don't be so dumb." So now I'm saying okay, okay, I'm yessing him like this just to get him off my ear. So Dickey is on him (Chandler), now he's on the way back. Now, he's maybe from here maybe ten feet from the home plate and Ted grabs me by the sleeve and he says, he says, "You know damn well they're not going to walk you to get to me."

And I said, oh man. So now, Chandler gets ready, ball one, strike one, ball two, here comes that hard sinker and Red Rolfe was playing fifteen feet in front of the bag. So there's that hard sinker and I knew what he was trying to do with me. He threw that sinker out there and I just go, base hit to left field. Conroy scored and Dominic had a good jump from second, we get two. Now, Williams is the next hitter. And Chandler is walking around the mound and he's just chewing me out to a fare-thee-well, and I'm not even looking at him.

I'm looking at Ted outside the batter's box. He's got a big grin and points to me, he says, listen to me, dummy. So Chandler is still giving me the devil. So to make a long story short, he gets up on the rubber, he steps off, and he gives me another blast and I told him where to go and I says, besides that, you were a lousy tipper in the Coast League. So now, he gets ready to pitch to Ted, the first pitch, Ted hits it.

He hits it 450 feet above the triangle in right center field. Of course, with two outs I'm running. I'm in the dugout moving; it's one of those balls that you hit that sounds like a gun going off. So I'm in the dugout, I think Bobby was sitting next to me and all the guys got up to see where the ball was going. And they all said, "Boy, Ted, you've got it all," and no one said nothing to me. I'm sitting in the dugout. I put us ahead. So everybody said, "Boy, Ted."

He goes, "Yeah, I hit that pretty darn good," he said. "Where is that horn-nosed little shortstop of ours?" And here he comes. He says, "Johnny, didn't I tell you how to hit Chandler?"

I said, "Ted, let me tell you something. He was so damn mad at

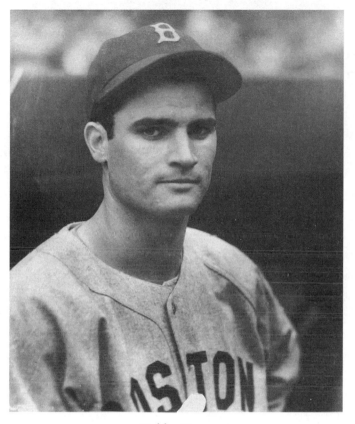

Bobby Doerr

me for getting that dinky little single he forgot you were the next hitter."

And Williams would hold court. And we'd listen. Here's a guy, when I got there he hit the .400. So we're sitting there and he's talking about so-and-so, well he does this, and you've got to get the ball, and you've got to get the ball when it comes out of his hand, and he says, you've got to watch, you've got to hit strikes, he says. My God, if you're a lousy hitter, you're going to be a lousy hitter. He says, but, he was always after, he loved Bobby (Doerr) and he used to tell Bobby, right after we got back after the war, we're in Boston, we got off to a great start that year. And for some reason Bobby is struggling.

I think we were about 40 and 10 after 50 games. Williams was hitting .600. Dom was hitting .400. I was hitting .400. (Rudy) York was hitting about .390. Well anyway, it's in May and we're waiting to take bat, and there was Dom, Bobby, and myself were in the dugout and Ted was down canvas alley getting his picture taken for a magazine article. So here comes Ted, he took it, now we're waiting to get on the field, and he says to Bobby, "Get up here," I can hear him, like it was yesterday.

He says, "Bobby," he says, "you're holding your bat up here, out here, open stance, closed stance, feet, what the heck's the matter with you." And Bobby hadn't said anything. This went on for about three or four minutes. He gave him a real dialogue is what he was about; he was giving him hitting instructions is what he was giving him.

And Bobby hadn't opened his mouth, and he says, and finally Bobby says, he says, "But, Ted, I'm not you."

Ted throws his arms up and he said, "You want to be a lousy .280 hitter, be a lousy .280 hitter."

He only hit 30 home runs that year and drove in 120-some runs. But he was amazing and a lot of times when you went to Ted if you were serious, he would sit and talk to you. And we always had a good rapport.

I thought I'd have to go into the service in July in '42. But Ted and I and Johnny Sain and Buddy Grimp and Joe Coleman all went into a flight program, and they told us that we wouldn't get called until the end of October. So we got into that and I knew nothing about flying. I followed Williams around like a little puppy dog and he said to me, "Come on, we'll get into, we'll get to finish the year." And I said, oh great.

So sure enough, it was true. We got to finish the year but they said from, toward the end of October, they even said November 1, we wouldn't get called. But two weeks after the season, we were in. And we went up to Amherst, Massachusetts, for what they called WTS, War Training Service. And from there we went to Chapel Hill, Chapel Hill to flight school. Ted went on to Pensacola. He got his wings. And I went to operations school, got my commission as an operations officer.

You know God gives so much to some people where he doesn't to others. And Ted worried about—we went in the Navy together and he worried more about me than he did himself. And we're flying in Indiana after we left Chapel Hill. And he's in one wing and I'm in another. And I'd seen him at five o'clock to eat. Then at seven o'clock I went down to get a little extra instruction in code, semaphore, and navigation.

I wasn't the best student in the world. So I'm there and Ted's hanging, and I'd say, "Well, I'll see you later. I'll see you tomorrow, Ted. Good luck, do your small field procedure perfectly."

And so he grabs me, and he says, "For crying out loud, Johnny, why can't you get this?" He says, "You've got a high school diploma not like me."

And I said, "But gee, Ted, I'm not you." I says, "You've got a great mind, I have to work hard."

And he said, "Well," he says, "when you learn something you retain it." He says, "I might forget it." So there's a left-handed compliment was what that was. But he was, he was so great.

My first big league contract was for $4,000 and I was happy to get it. I knew I was going to go in the Navy.

So two weeks is left of the season and there's a note on my chair and I had the locker next to Ted and Dom and Bobby were, we were like this, all four of us were always together. Well anyway, Ted sees the note on my chair and said, "What's that?"

And I said, "I don't know."

So he said, "Well, let's see what it is."

And I got to go up, and it says go up and see Mr. Collins.

He said, "What did you do?"

I said, "What do you mean, what did I—"

So I go upstairs. So Ted says to me, he says, "Hurry up and come back, we'll go out and eat."

I said, "Okay." I know he's waiting down there. So I go into Collins's office. He sets me down and he says, "Johnny," he says, "you know, I know you're getting ready to go, the season is at an end, you're going to have to go in the Navy. We hope this thing don't last too long," he says, "but I want you to know that, you know, you had a fine year, you didn't give us any trouble on the field or off the field." He says, "Mr. Yawkey wanted me to give you this."

It's an envelope, brown envelope. Boston Red Sox, 4 Yawkey Way. So I don't even open it. And I'm trying to get away from Collins and Collins is giving me a little dialogue about behavior and all this. So now I finally leave and Williams is waiting for me.

And he says, "Where in the heck have you been?"

And I said, "Well, I was talking with Collins."

"What's this in your hand?"

"He gave me this."

And he says, "Well, open it." Williams always did everything with a flair so I opened it and it was a check. He said, "Well, what is it?"

I said, "It says $5,000 here." Five thousand.

And he says, "It's a bonus."

Pretty good, and we got $1,100 out of the World Series that year too, and when I sent it home, my parents thought I stole it somewhere. What I did, I took my oldest brother, we put everything together to take care of our folks. But this five grand was a down payment on a house out in Oregon. And my brother still lives in it.

When we were on the trains a lot we kind of sat together because we liked to talk about pitching and what this guy did. And a lot of times Ted would say, "Well, wait till you see this guy." You know, you know. And they tell that old story about when Bobby (Doerr) said that to Ted. He said, "Wait'll you see Jimmie Foxx."

And Ted turned to Bobby and said, "Wait'll Foxx sees me." There was a little gag about that years ago. But it's true. But Jimmie liked Ted. I got pictures of that. I think there's some still around the ballpark where there's this skinny little guy and Fox being so muscular.

Foxx was, he wasn't six-two, but he was as strong as an ox. I think if I had to compare the two, I'd probably compare him to Vern Stephens in body build, but I think Foxx might have been stronger. Foxx for his size, you know, you look at him and say, well this guy can't run but he could run.

Jimmie Foxx

Oh, and I remember we were going down to Washington and it was an overnight and we had the upper berth and the lower berth, and being a rookie I had to go to the upper berth. So I grabbed up and I could jump in and go to bed. And he come by and he says, "What's the matter, kid, are you having trouble?" And he got me under the buttocks and pushed me.

He was very strong and a very nice man. Jeez, was he a nice guy. And every time we'd go into Chicago or Detroit or St. Louis or New York or Washington or Philly, then Ted would say, "Well, this is where Foxx hit one."

And I said, "Oh, you've got to be kidding me."

And he says, "Johnny, believe me." What Williams said, we always took as gospel truth.

I loved Dom. I loved Bob. But Dom and I were more compatible to one another then because Bobby and Ted came first and then Dom and then me. And we—they said, here are the fearless foursome from the West Coast. We're the fearless foursome, but we got on Ted's coattails and he knew how to handle it. I thought Ted Williams was the smartest guy I've ever known. When he went into the Navy, he went through that program like a graduate from MIT. So bright, so academically smart, with a high school diploma.

This play happened in the eighth inning in Game 7 of the '46 World Series. There were two outs. Harry Walker was the hitter, a left-handed hitter. And Slaughter's on first base. And as—between the shortstop and second baseman, of course, Bobby (Doerr) being the elder statesmen, he gives the signs. So he gave me the sign. So I'm covering. So now sure enough, I'm covering and here comes Enos. He's coming in there like a—he didn't even—he had the base—he was only maybe eight or ten feet away from the bag when I got there. He was stealing. And the ball in the meantime is hit to left center field. And he just turned and he went through. Mike Gonzalez tried to hold him up at third, but they're telling me, but my back was turned, and I had to go out. I went out in left field maybe forty, fifty feet. And I'd have needed a gun to get him. When I picked him up he was about ten feet from home plate. But nobody said anything and I couldn't hear.

So now Arch McDonald, the great announcer from Washington, put a pair of horns on me. And there were a few catcalls, stuff like that. "Aw, you bum," and all this. But you learn to live with them.

At first I was a little sensitive to it. But I'll tell you what happened. My wife and I went back, well, she had met my folks and we went back (to Oregon) after that series. And we're at a football game between Oregon and Oregon State College. And we're up in stands and the game is going and it's raining cats and dogs, as they say. No scoring in the first half, bad handling of the ball, fumbling and all this, recovering and everything. Now we go underneath for coffee, under the stands and get coffee. And my wife is there, a couple of my friends, and coming into our row, a drunk, two rows behind us spots me. And he says, "Pesky, you bum. What'd you hold the ball for?" Oh.

So my wife says, "I thought the people out here were nice."

I said, "Look at this. They have every right to say that. They believe that, let them."

She said, "I thought the people were nice here."

I said, "Let me tell you something, kiddo. If I'd a' stayed in Boston, I'd been hanging in the Boston Common."

So he finally—the two teams come back on the field and I think that year Oregon State was the favorite and they kicked off to Oregon and first play from scrimmage, they fumble the ball and recover their own fumble. They line up again, the guy fumbles the ball. Oregon State recovers. And the drunk gets up and he says, "Aw, give the ball to Pesky. He knows how to hold it." So you live with that.

They used to say in Boston, who's better than his brother Joe? Dominic DiMaggio. And he could field every bit as good. He ran as good. Joe was a good runner. Dominic was good. They had great baseball instincts. Dominic had as good baseball instincts as anybody that I've been around in all the years I've seen the game.

In the outfield he kind of stood there, straddled. I mean, three-quarters one way. But he could go back on the ball. You swear to God, you look out there and you say, "Jeez, he's a little shallow, isn't he?" When the ball's hit you look up and say, "He'll never catch that." Two steps and he's under the ball.

He was as good a defensive outfielder as anybody's that's ever played the game. They talk about (Willie) Mays and they talk about (Roberto) Clemente, but you've got to throw Dominic in there. I would. I've been blowing his horn for ten years—twenty years. I hope he'll make the Hall of Fame one of these days.

The years that we played, you would go into New York, you'd look at Reynolds, Raschi, Lopat, Tommy Byrne. You went to Cleveland you look at Feller, Lemon, Wynn, Garcia, and then you had those two guys out of the bullpen, Narleski and Mossi.

And when you went across the lake to Detroit you looked at

Trucks, Trout, and Newhouser. Boy, again, when you played against those guys, you always went to Ted. If you hit, he'd ask Dom, say, "How is this guy throwing?" Yeah, you say, "Well, you've got to be ready. He's got a little extra today," or whatever. Like he asked Bobby, Bobby would hit a home run and Ted would say, "What did you hit, a curveball, a fastball?"

He says, "I don't know."

Then he'd throw his arms up and he'd give him a dialogue that would burn you.

I hit so few home runs that I can remember every one that I ever hit. See, I only hit 17 in ten years. But see, the right field pole in Boston's only 295, but in the old Yankee Stadium before they fixed it up it was even less than that.

Parnell started that Pesky Pole stuff. The funny thing, he was, well, we're all through playing and he's through pitching and he's doing—working on radio and TV with (Jerry) Coleman and (Ned) Martin. And somebody hit a home run down there late in the ball game right around the pole and Parnell come up and he said, "Well, we used to call that Pesky's Pole." And he said, "Well, he won a ball game for me with a home run so we called it Pesky." And that's how it started. And other announcers like Trupiano and Castiglione kind of picked it up. And it's kind of flattering to me. And people go to the ballpark and take pictures of that and I get mail to sign the doggone pole.

I'll remember this. There's this thing where Larry Doby walked by Ted. And I think Larry even said this publicly. He says, "I walked by Ted Williams and Ted says, 'Good luck, kid.'" You know. Now he didn't have to say that. But Ted was very fond of some of those black players. He thought Willie Mays was ice cream, you know. He loved Mays—Clemente—(Willie) Stargell—

I saw Satchel Paige play in Portland. I was a kid; I was in high school. And working around the ballpark and when the Kansas City Monarchs came into town they'd have 8,000, 10,000, 15,000 people. And he's putting on this act but he could really fire. Now I don't know whether he did this—got involved with the whole team, but he'd have the infielders all sit down. And he'd just whew! And they were trying to hit him. I think maybe two guys fouled balls off. And Josh (Gibson) would always catch one inning in a rocking chair.

The greatest ballplayers I ever saw were DiMaggio, Mays, Williams the greatest hitter, but for overall ability I'd have to say Mays.

My number one manager was Ralph Houk. I had great admiration for him. He knew the game. And he was a tough cookie.

A guy I thought was a good manager was Don Zimmer. I thought he should've never left Boston. There's Kevin Kennedy. Kevin Kennedy was a good manager. Good everyday manager. Danny Murtaugh, when I was over with the Pirates for a few years. I think Jimy Williams—I like what he did because baseball has changed so much. You've got a different type of athlete playing this game now. You've got more personality. You've got the Latin kids; you've got the black kids; you've got the white kids. And you've got to be fair to all of them. I like Tony LaRussa. Of course if you don't like Joe Torre, you don't like yourself. He's great. But you see, Joe has run the gauntlet.

Red Sox catcher number one in my book was Carlton Fisk, big strong guy. Johnny Bench with Cincinnati was another. Berra is another. Roy Campanella. Elston Howard is another one. He would go back and see it all. Lance Parrish. I liked him, too. But if I had to pick one guy, I'd have to pick two or three probably. Of course, I saw Dickey at the end of his career. But I'd have to say Fisk and Bench would be, would be my guys. For everything: catching, running, and so on. Fisk was a good athlete. In fact, he ran better than Johnny Bench.

At first base I'd have to pick Foxx. I had only a couple of months with him but I thought my next would be either Walt Dropo—I thought Dropo was a hell of a player. My second baseman, of course, is Bobby—Bobby Doerr. Shortstop is Luis Aparicio. We had him for a couple of years. Third baseman has to be Wade Boggs. And my hitting shortstop would be Nomar Garciaparra—Aparicio for everything. For hitting, he didn't hit a lot. Of course, if you were to make the comparison of the two, Garciaparra probably had more power. But Aparicio was outstanding. He had a fine arm. Everything was right like a pitcher from off the mound. I never saw him ever throw a ball away.

The best pitchers? I'd have to say Pedro Martinez and Roger Clemens. Feller. Warren Spahn, yeah. Sandy Koufax and Spahn. Bob Gibson. Allie Reynolds was the guy I was thinking about. I always had a soft spot for him.

I'll never forget when Casey brought Whitey Ford into a game in Fenway. And he'd had all these scoreless innings and everything. And I think there was one out. I'm the hitter, then Ted. And Ted is on the on-deck, I'm—he grabbed me, he said, "Watch this guy, watch this guy. We heard a lot about this guy. Watch how he throws." So I'm watching and Whitey was right there. But I think the second pitch I hit up the middle. And Williams hit one in the alley or something.

So I said to Ted in the dugout, I say, "What do you think of that little left-hander?"

He said, "He's pretty damn good." You could go to Ted, you know, and he would never lie to you about a guy. He says if you—if he had something that somebody else didn't have, he'd say well, this guy's got a little bit more than this guy. He'd always make a comparison between the two. But Ted could judge that way. Because that's the kind of mind he had.

I wish I was blessed with more talent, but I used every bit of thing that I had and tried as hard as I could, and played as hard as I could and hustled as hard as I could. And I see some old-timers come up and say, "Well, we saw you play." And there's a pause. "Because you always hustled." And that's what I did. I tried to do that. I insisted on that because when you have limited ability, not being a big man. I had no power; I hit the ball; I ran hard; I played hard. And I just want to—if someone is good enough to say I was a decent man and I had a great love for the game of baseball.

WARREN SPAHN

The game of baseball has seen its share of great left-handed pitchers—including Lefty Grove, Steve Carlton, Randy Johnson, Whitey Ford, Carl Hubbell, Sandy Koufax, and Rube Waddell—but Warren Spahn may well have been the greatest of them all.

If hitting is timing and pitching is upsetting timing, as Warren Spahn once said, then the great southpaw hurler left thousands of batters wondering what had gone wrong.

Spahn spent a long and distinguished career as a starting pitcher, mostly with the Braves, first in Boston and then in Milwaukee, ending his 21 major league seasons (1942, 1946–1965) as the winningest left-hander in history with 363 victories. Despite losing three years to his military service in World War II, Spahn's longevity would allow him to put up mind-boggling numbers—winning 20 or more games 13 times (including six years in a row), tossing 63 shutouts, leading the National League in complete games nine times, victories eight times, and strikeouts four times, and completing 382 of his 665 career starts.

"He was the greatest left-handed pitcher to ever put on a uniform. Just think how many games he would have won if he hadn't been in the Army," said Johnny Logan, a teammate of Spahn's with the Braves. "His success was knowing the opponents' weaknesses. That's what made Spahnie so great."

Hall of Fame pitcher Bob Feller, himself one of the game's great hurlers and an opponent of Spahn's in the 1948 World Series, said, "In my mind, he was the greatest left-hander of all time."

Warren Spahn

Spahn, a big league pitcher until he was forty-four, would address the pitcher's dilemma when he said, "What is life, after all, but a challenge? And what better challenge can there be than the one between the pitcher and the hitter." He would also remark, "A pitcher needs two pitches, one they're looking for and one to cross them up."

MY DAD WAS AN AMATEUR BALLPLAYER, and he loved the game. And of course, his son played baseball. Well, in those days it was during the Depression, and I didn't even have a left-handed glove. I had a right-handed glove—one of his, and I didn't know the thumb was supposed to be on this side, so I played with a glove that had the thumb over here.

And I guess, I learned how to catch with it maybe better than kids do today, because they've got the big long gloves and all that sort of thing. And it was a love affair. I enjoyed playing baseball. I played in a great municipal league that they had in Buffalo along with my high school, American Legion ball. I think I was playing almost every day. I wanted to be a first baseman because I was left-handed. And my father played third base, and I played first base on the same ball club, the South Bethel Businessmen's—whatever. And I used to give him heck for throwing me bad throws, and he'd give me heck for not catching the ones that he threw badly, that, you know, I was a first baseman. I was supposed to catch those. And we had a good relationship, and baseball was the catalyst that made it closer together as father and son.

When I went to high school, the young man that was playing first base for my high school was an All-High first baseman. So I realized that I wasn't going to beat him out, and they needed pitching, and that's when I started to pitch. And interestingly my wife and Stan Musial's wife both agreed that when he went from pitcher to the outfield and I went from first base to pitching, we made the right decision, and I guess we did, because Stan did pretty well.

That distinctive high kick I had was part of my father's influence. Use all of the momentum that I could create. And then listening to hitters, I realized that I hid the ball pretty well so that it looked like it was coming out of my uniform, so I tried to encourage that. I didn't want to talk to pitchers. I wanted to talk to hitters. And I think hitters are the same way. So over the years, I realized where the assets were and embellished on it.

And Johnny Cooney, who was an outfielder and a coach with us—we didn't have coaches. They were just part-time—whatever. And Johnny Cooney was the pitching coach, and he told me that I shouldn't raise my right shoulder like I did when I pitched—that I'd lose sight of home plate, et cetera, and whatever, but I could never break that habit. And I think another interesting thing about my delivery is that when I was in high school, I played football and

I was an end. Two guys and I landed on my right shoulder and dislocated my shoulder. And as a result, I couldn't throw it up in the air like a lot of pitchers do, so I kept it tucked inside, which happened to be the right thing to do.

I think the philosophy that I used was that the fifteen inches in the middle of the plate belong to the hitter, and that the two and a half inches or two inches on either side is where you have to pitch. And when you stop to think about it, a hitter goes up to home plate, and he takes a stance to protect most of the strike zone or what he is comfortable with, so you pitch against that grain.

I never saw a major league game until I played in one. But I heard about Lefty Grove, Herb Pennock, Carl Hubbell, but I didn't get to see them. Of course, we got the radio broadcasts of the Yankee games. So I knew of those people. And I got to hit against Carl Hubbell when he was at the Giants and I was at the Braves when I first came up.

And I remember hitting against him. First of all, you're looking for him to break the ball away from you, and he threw me that screwball that was bigger than any right-hander's curveball. It looked goofy coming from a left-hander, and then break in on me like that. So that influenced me a great deal. And, you know, I guess I idolized guys like Lou Gehrig, for example. I never saw Lou play; I never got to meet him, but I idolized him. He was the opposite of Babe Ruth. He was a good-looking guy. He looked like Tarzan, and so he was my idol when I was a kid.

I experimented. And I don't think I had the greatest curveball in the world, but I had a quick breaking ball. I remember Larry Doby had a lot of trouble with me in the World Series in '48. And he came up to me one day and said, "What is that pitch?" And after I told him, he hit me better than he did before. You know, he caught me. But I had a quick curveball, and I was able to throw it on the outside corner to the right-handed hitters.

In fact, Willie Mays hit his first home run off me, and his first hit in the big leagues was that very same curveball that Robin Roberts had pitched against him. They had a series with the Phillies in the beginning of the year, and I think Willie was, like, 0-for-23, and he was worried about getting sent down. So I was told that he couldn't handle a curveball on the outside part of the plate, but they forgot to tell me that was from a right-hander. And he knocked a couple of seats out in the Polo Grounds. And that was Willie's first hit. You don't forget those things.

I went into baseball right out of high school but I never dreamed that I was going to be a professional, and when I got that opportunity, I grabbed it. And I remember that the guys that were graduating out of high school with me were making, like, $15, $17 a week working in the steel mills, and I was making $20 playing Class D baseball, so I was delighted to play baseball, number one, and make more money than those guys did.

I had a scholarship to Cornell, but it was only books and tuition, or maybe just books; I don't remember. And my family couldn't afford to send me to college, so I thought this is an opportunity to make money after I got out of high school. And I thought if there was anything in my future as far as college was concerned, I would take that up at a later date.

I only knew one scout, and I think he was a bird-dog for the Braves. And he worked for the New York Central Railroad. And he offered me a contract, which I grabbed. And after that, I think I had inquiries from the Yankees and whatever that they wanted to sign me, but I had already signed with the Braves. And, you know, to make it sensible in my own mind, I thought, "Well, I made a good decision, because if I was going to get to the big leagues, I would have an opportunity to do it with the Braves rather than the Yankees," because I remember the Yankees when they had a great ball club in Newark, and could have competed with the Yankees in the big leagues.

In the minors I got the bright idea that I was going to throw a curveball that would break late, and instead of getting my fingers on top of the ball, I tried to throw it this way. And when I did, I hurt my elbow. And the ball club sent me to a chiropractor somewhere outside of Bradford, Pennsylvania, where I was playing, I remember, and this guy manipulated my elbow, and I thought he was tearing it apart.

And apparently a tendon had slipped from one place to an-other, and he put that back in place. And he put my arm in a sling, told me to go home and forget baseball for the rest of that year. And he wouldn't even let me comb my hair with my left arm. I think that was really a break because the Braves organization sent me to Evansville, where Bob Coleman was the manager, who was an outstanding teacher, and I never had trouble with my elbow again.

I wanted to play every day, and I wanted to be good enough to maybe play another position. This is where the first base came in. I wanted to be a better hitter than the guy that Fred Haney or any other manager—Billy Southworth—had on the bench to pinch-hit for him. So it helped. There were situations where I stayed in the ball game where maybe another pitcher wouldn't, because I had potential. And I wasn't a good hitter, but I was a dangerous out.

What else have you got to do when you only go out there to pitch every fourth day or now it's five days. So you watch other people, and the mistakes that they make. I'd like to be one step ahead of them. I wasn't the biggest guy in the world, so instead of brawn, you try to think your way through situations. And I think it helped me in my career.

After you pitched a game, you'd run your butt off the next day. This was a Coleman influence and maybe my dad that, you know, there are poisons that are developed in your system when you use muscles so that you have stiffness. The only way that you're going to get rid of that stiffness is through your blood system, so if you sweat, you get rid of some of that stuff. And we were taught to run, run, run, run, run, and the day after I pitched, I would run my tail off in the outfield.

And then the second day, you'd throw batting practice, and I think that was good because you concentrate on control, getting the ball where you want to get it or you let the guy hit it, but it's es-tablishing that rhythm to get the ball in the strike zone. And then the third day, I don't think I threw a whole lot, but then I was ready to pitch again.

I know that many people said, "Don't do what Spahn does." I

Casey Stengel

used to throw from the outfield like an outfielder just to stretch my arm out, but I knew it was good for me. And managers say, "Don't do what that silly son of a gun does," but I never had a sore arm.

I can remember when I first came up to the big leagues, Braves Field was a pretty old stadium, but that was the big leagues to me. And when I first pitched in the big leagues, I thought, "Wow! Those guys are big leagues and I wonder if I have to change the way I pitch."

I was with the Braves in '42, briefly. And we were playing the Dodgers, and the Dodgers always beat the devil out of us. And the Dodgers also got our signs from second base and relayed them to the hitter. And I remember that Casey Stengel, the Braves' manager, was going to have a switch, and one was going to be the curveball and two the fastball. And Pee Wee Reese was the hitter. We were going to retaliate for them getting the signs from second base.

And Casey gave me the sign for the knockdown pitch, and I threw inside, and I think I threw back here, and Pee Wee just moved his head out of the way. And Casey jumped up, and when he did, he hit his head on the top of the dugout, which was concrete. Now, he's real mad. And he gave me the knockdown again, and I threw here and missed him, so Casey came out to the mound, and he said, "Young man, you don't have any guts. I ought to send you to Hartford to get some." I was gone the next day. So I finished the season in Hartford.

Casey was a great showman. He was a great ambassador for baseball. Casey would stay up all night as long as there was somebody in the lobby of the hotel to hear his stories. And he was a great double-talker, so that you had to hang with him, because you didn't know what he was talking about. And he would be up early in the morning to talk to whoever wanted to talk baseball again.

I think he was a very clever manager. I think Casey probably was one of the people that started switching left versus right and right versus left. I think that he cultivated Allie Reynolds as a starter and a reliever. He used to get Hank Bauer so crazy, because he wanted to play every day, and he knew just exactly when Hank Bauer was just about to go over the edge, and then he would put him in the ball game.

Casey Stengel told me this many years ago. And he said, "You ought to be very proud of your father."

And I said, "Well, I am."

He said my father came back after the ball game, and he grabbed Casey, who is a pretty big man; my father was a little guy—grabbed him by the front of his shirt, and he, kind of, beat the heck out of him, because he sent me down to Hartford. And he said, "Now, who has no guts?"

And Casey himself told me that story, and my father never said anything about that. But that's the pride that my dad had in me and, kind of like I couldn't afford to let him down.

Well, when I was a rookie and went to spring training, Paul Waner was my roommate. And Paul was a maverick, so I guess not too many people wanted to room with him. And he used to come to spring training in an old beat-up Model A, and he would have his fishing equipment there rather than his baseball stuff. And in the morning, we woke up, and we had to be at the ballpark, and we had to walk to the ballpark. That was part of our training. And Paul reached under his bed and grabbed a pint, and he took a sip, and, I guess, my eyeballs went through the roof, because I didn't think ballplayers should do that.

But anyway, Paul recognized that and he said, "Now look," he says, "this is our secret." And he says, "I have astigmatism." And he said, "If I don't have a drink before I go to the ballpark, I see two balls, and I don't know which one to hit." He said, "But when I have a drink, then I see one big ball." And I think maybe Paul might have believed that.

I remember Ernie Lombardi, who was one of the catchers that I pitched to, and again traits—I was taught to waste a pitch, and I remember I threw a pitch outside to Ernie, and he was so big and clumsy that instead of catching the ball with the glove, he stuck his bare hand out and caught. And he chewed tobacco, and he spit on the ball and rubbed it up, and he threw a sidearm to me harder than I threw it to him.

And I thought, "If that's the way catchers throw in the big league, I don't belong." So I think success—which comes first, the chicken or the egg? And I think you have to be successful before you're confident, and you have to be confident to be successful. So they're hand in hand. So I think you develop those things as you go along. And I remember the first ball game I won in the big leagues. I was on high cotton. I was on cloud nine. I felt that the world was my oyster and that I couldn't wait to get back out there.

Well, I remember when war was declared, and I certainly was eligible, and I certainly felt that I was going to be drafted, and I was scared to death. I didn't want to go. I didn't want to be a soldier, but I was drafted. And again, if I'm a soldier, I wanted to be the best soldier I could possibly be. If I'm a pitcher, I want to be the best pitcher I could be. So I think those traits fit along that same line.

And I remember when I was drafted, the recruiter said what did I do in civilian life, and I said I was a professional ballplayer. And he said, "What the heck are we going to do with you?" So they put me at the 14th Armored Division. If you were a truck driver, they made a baker out of you, and if you were a baker, they made you a truck driver. They wanted to teach you their way. And so I wound up in the 14th Armored Division, and then the Army streamlined the armor division, and I was in D Company, and they streamlined it to headquarters A, B, and C Company.

So they took all the people in D Company and established the Combat Engineer Battalions, and E Company was a bridge company, so they made a separate unit. At any rate, I wound up as a combat engineer, and a combat engineer is one that digs holes and does all the dirty work that nobody else wants to do.

I remember one time we were surrounded by the Germans I think at Bastogne (in Belgium). And I remember that the password we had among us was who played the keystone sack for the Dodgers? Well, any German wouldn't know that. That was American lingo, and God help the guy that didn't know who played second base for the Dodgers.

You didn't know if the guy next to you was German or American. The Germans had all of our uniforms. They had our dog tags. They had our equipment.

Well, our orders were to go to the Rhine River, and we were trying to establish a way to get across the Rhine River. And our orders—my battalion is to go to the Rhine River and stop. And I think, and I'm only surmising, that it was an agreement that the Russians were going to go into Berlin first. And all of a sudden, here's this bridge that had just a skeleton crew on.

And that I found out later that the Germans had put demolitions on that bridge to blow it up, and they didn't go off. So we just shot the heck out of those Germans that were on that bridge and took it. And we established a bridgehead about fifty yards, I think, beyond that bridge. And now what do we do? "Hey, we need help."

And the purpose of—well, our purpose was to put treadway across—that was a railroad bridge, and our job was to put treadway across there to get our troops and our tanks across there.

And the Germans knew exactly what we were doing. And the minute we started working, it was like the Fourth of July, that they threw everything at us. And there were planes that were swooping down over that bridge dropping bombs and then disappear over another bridge at the other side. And we set up our artillery and machine gun fire. And every fifth bullet, I think, was a tracer or maybe it was more.

But at any rate, it looked like the whole sky was lit up with those tracers, and you know, that was only one of five. And I remember a P-38 that the Germans had captured, and this pilot was flying and he was shot down, and the front end of that P-38 was big and long.

And it went straight down into the ground. And we went to capture this guy or what was left, and the plane burned so that he was nothing but charcoal. You couldn't touch him; he would just fall apart. And it's just an illustration as to: The Germans had our equipment, our uniforms, our dog tags, whatever. They were well prepared. But, you know, they didn't have the American pride and the gung ho thing that the Americans had. But we held the bridge. And our job was to get it ready for getting our tanks and men across, and we added so much weight to that bridge that it fell apart. And I remember I was an officer talking to another guy that I had relieved that he had people stationed in strategic places for protection. And we were going over those things and all of a sudden, we were at the east side of the bridge at the abutment, and it was, like, machine gun fire. And, you know, we all went down on the ground or whatever. It was the rivets popping out of that bridge and that's when that thing fell. [That was the bridge at Remagen.]

We held that area, and then we got a pontoon bridge across the Rhine that would suffice until we got some more bridges across there to the north and the south of this.

When I came back after the Army, I thought, "Wow, if I don't do well, nobody's going to shoot me." I for one was that thankful that

I had the travesty of the service to fall back on, and bases loaded and Musial hitting—it wasn't as important a fact.

Well, let me say this, the guy that pitched before I went in the service was a different guy than the guy that came back. My confidence level was so much better. Again, which comes first: the chicken or the egg? I felt that I could do my job. And my son was born in 1948, and I felt like I couldn't afford to lose. I couldn't afford to fail. You know, that's the responsibility I felt.

There were ten pitchers on the ball club. And we had four maybe five people that were starters, and the other people were in the bullpen. Well, I wanted to be one of those starters, because I wanted to be a guy that played every day, and I couldn't do that. And you sort of feel like you were a part of the ball club when you're a starting pitcher.

My first win in the big leagues, I was hoping it would be in the Polo Grounds. And this is before I went in the service. They had a deal at the Polo Ground where kids could get in the ballpark with, like, five pounds of scrap metal. And in the seventh inning, all the ushers went home and the kids all came down in the lower part of the grandstand, and then they came out on the field to get autographs. And we were behind at the time, and the loudspeaker said that if they didn't get off the field that they were going to forfeit the game to the Braves.

Well, I was the pitcher of record when that did happen, and I remember Babe Barna hit a double off me into left center field. At any rate, we were behind and now we won the game 7-to-nothing, because of the forfeit. And I was hoping that I'd get the win. But all the records, the hitters and their times at bat and whatever, counted, but the pitcher's records didn't count. So I didn't get my first victory.

After the war I felt we had a contending ball club. I had a good year in 1947. I think I had an ERA that was, like, 2.33. Ralph Branca and I won 20 ball games. He beat me out of the top pitcher award—I remember that. It was a stepping-stone for the rest of my career, and I felt that I belonged; I felt that I was a part of the starting rotation.

And being successful doesn't hurt. So that was a great year for me personally, and also I think for the Braves that this was the nucleus to the ball club that won the pennant the following year in '48. We had a bunch of old guys, though.

I didn't have a real good year in 1948. I won 15 and I lost 12. But I pitched in a lot of ball games where I was pinch-hit for or was relieved in the later part of the game, but we were in a pennant fight. And we also had guys by the name of Nelson Potter and Bobby Hogue that were good relievers, so I think that was indicative. And I think the interesting thing about that was that my ERA in '48 was identical to another year when I won 20. So, you know, we had a good defensive ball club—a double play combination, center field, pitching, and we were in a lot of ball games that we weren't the year before.

Every game was important, and when we played the Dodgers, they were doubly important because the difference of a game in a winning column and a loss column. Yeah, I remember one year that the Dodgers started out 22-3, and we were winning, and yet, we were like eight games behind, because they got off to such a great start. But they had a good organization.

They had good instructors in their organization. And they also had some good talent. And I remember when we got center fielder Sam Jethroe. I remember Branch Rickey saying we stole the best prospect they had in the Dodger organization. Bull. They knew he couldn't see, and he ran on his heels. And I saw that guy run right by fly balls, that he ran so hard it took them ten minutes to retrieve the ball after he ran by. But, you know, they knew what they had.

In the 1948 World Series I pitched the second game, and I pitched again in the fifth game. And I threw the ball better in the fifth game than I did in the second game. But Cleveland had a good ball club. And then, let's see, the sixth game: That one draws a blank. But we got beat in six games. Oh, Gene Bearden, that son of a gun couldn't do any wrong, and I think he came in and relieved and they won the sixth game.

Well, I felt that we were the big leagues and we played a World Series. So if we played a World Series, then we should be able to play against the best of every nation: black, white, yellow, green, or whatever. And Jackie Robinson was a good talent. He could run like a deer. What tickled me was that we heard about Jackie, and Branch Rickey picked the first black guy in baseball because of his college education, because of his athleticism. And I understand from other black people that the catcher in the Negro Leagues Josh Gibson was a better ballplayer than Jackie. But Jackie fit the mold that Branch Rickey wanted to break the color line with.

I wanted the catcher to give me a location. If the catcher gives me a fastball, I'd go up and in; yeah, I'd like that. Then there's another place for the fastball and that's down and away. So if I didn't like going inside on this hitter, I would just stare him off, and then he'd go outside. So it didn't matter what pitch he'd call for, but it was important about the location of it. And also, one pitch sets up another one.

You know, change-of-speed, like, I think is almost a lost art in baseball; it's coming back a little bit. But the breaking ball is a different speed than the fastball, and the change should be a different speed than the curveball. So now, the hitter has got three options as to how quickly he strides and how quick he has to be with his hands. And every hitter is an egotist. You throw a fastball by a hitter, and boy, he's going to be reared up to hit that next one.

And if you change up on him, he screws himself in the ground. I think this is the attitude I had when I was pitching is that I could nullify any hitter that came up there. And it wasn't with throwing a ball by him, but changing speeds. I was a better pitcher against a right-hander.

The hitters will tell you a story. I don't know. And I know that if I threw a fastball by a hitter, I was throwing pretty good. And if I threw my curveball, and they swung over the top, that was pretty good, too.

At Cooperstown we'd have our dinner and everybody would get up and speak as went around. And Ted Williams got up and he said all pitchers are stupid. And about twelve or thirteen of those people were pitchers. I was about the third person that spoke after

Ted, and I said, "Well, Ted, if all these pitchers are stupid, how come you only hit .406? Fifty percent is .500, and you didn't hit that."

And, of course, I loved to argue with Ted, because he loved to talk baseball and he loved to argue. And I used to deliberately get him to talk about hitting just to hear him. And the older that Ted got, the greater a hitter he was when he was playing. And that thing in Cooperstown where you showed batting averages and where the ball was located in the strike zone, all through the strike zone. Ted is one of my favorite people and a student of the game.

I pitched against him in the All-Star Game in Chicago in 1947, and the count went to 3-and-2, and I threw Ted my curveball, and he took it for strike three. I didn't see Ted again until we played the City Series in Boston, and he came running out to left field where I was, and he said, "When did you start throwing a slider?" Well, I didn't throw a slider, but when the greatest hitter in baseball calls it a slider, I guess that's what it was. And he told me every pitch that I threw him during the time that he was at bat, and then got the 3-and-2 pitch that I threw in the curveball.

It amazed me that he knew every pitch I threw, and he said, "That fastball that you threw to me is pretty effective. You ought to use it more often." So now, we're playing the All-Star Game in Washington, D.C., and I remembered what Ted had said. And I had two strikes on him, and I threw him a fastball right here. And he hit it into the bleachers for a home run. And if you ever watched the pitcher during a ball game, when a guy hits a home run, he has nothing to do. He would pick up the rosin bag and throw it and whatever. Well, I happened to think about Ted, and I looked around at second base and I said, "You conned me, didn't you?"

And he did. You know, he used to spend the time that he wasn't hitting in a ball game looking through the hole in his cap, the little air hole, and watch the pitcher. He never watched anything else other than the pitcher, so that either they tipped pitches off, or he had a good idea about what they were going to throw him. So he was great, but he wasn't that great. He had some inside information.

•   •   •

In 1948 a writer in Boston coined that phrase "Spahn and Sain, and pray for rain." And the scheduling in New England in September and late in August, there is a lot of rain, and also, there is a lot off-days put in the schedule because of that. Well, it just so happened that during a course of three or four weeks that Sain would pitch, I would pitch and then it would rain. Day off, and then we'd come back and Sain and I.

And Vern Bickford was a great pitcher, and he didn't get a chance to pitch. And he hurt his arm at that time. So we were pitching every other game, John Sain and I. And this writer in Boston coined the phrase: "Spahn and Sain, and pray for rain." In the annals of baseball, there's only a few things like that, Tinker to Evers to Chance, the double play combination, and the great outfield of

Johnny Sain

Hooper, Speaker, and Lewis, and then here along comes pitching. And not Feller, not anybody else, but Spahn and Sain, and pray for rain. So I thought it was a great tribute.

This is one of the things I don't understand about baseball today, is that guys pitch once a week, they pitch five innings. They don't pitch in relief, they don't pitch batting practice. You know, to me your arm is like your legs; you've got to use them to keep them in shape. And how in the heck can these guys today stay off the disabled list with what little throwing they do? I threw more than anybody ever—I did all the things you shouldn't do as a pitcher. I threw in the outfield and whatever, but I did it for rhythm. I did it to feel making the ball stay on the same plane and backspin and whatever, so it helped me in my pitching.

You know, everything today is predicated on preventing a sore arm and the five-man rotation and counting the pitches. Well, we get more sore arms now than we ever had in history. And it's because pitchers never get their arms in shape. And how about the shortstops? How about the second baseman, the third baseman? They throw every day. Why doesn't a pitcher? And I think baseball has made cripples out of pitchers, or freaks, and I don't think it's right.

There was a little guy with Pittsburgh by the name of Curt Roberts. He probably hit me better than anybody in baseball. And, you know, it seemed like every time I raised my arm he got a base hit, and thank God the right-handers got him out of the league for me. I think it's the timing. I think it's the timing of the rhythm of the pitcher and the rhythm of the hitter swinging the bat. And there were a lot of good hitters that I had good luck with.

I used to watch the line scores of the games before I pitched against a ball club. And a lot of times the guy that was hot was the guy that you had to watch out for when the .300 hitter wasn't hitting or whatever. So that I knew who I could take liberties with and who I couldn't.

Well, Bob Feller came up before I did and I heard all the things about how hard he threw and whatever. And, you know, he was all those things. And he was a little bit past his prime when we played Cleveland in the World Series. But I've been with Bob and I've been in All-Star Games and whatever with him. And he's a very proud guy. And he talks about throwing his fastball faster than a racehorse could run.

Then they used the motorcycle to test how fast he ran. Of course, we didn't have the (Juggs) gun in those days, but Bob had a great curveball to go along with that fastball. And he was a work-horse, too. I used to love to see how he strutted around the mound. Arrogance personified.

The hitter tells you a story and, and if you don't throw it by him you, you back up third base. But, no, I think I relied on change-of-speeds more than Bob. As a matter of fact, I was Nolan Ryan's pitching coach at Anaheim when he was there and I tried to get him to throw his curveball and his change to set up his fastball. But Nolan had such a big ego, he wanted to strike people out instead of win.

And that's no reflection on Nolan per se, but just the art of pitching; I think guys have God-given talent like a Feller or a Ryan, and they overlook the fact that pitching is an art.

As I say, the hitter tells you a story, and if that story says that this guy can hit the ball from the middle of the plate in, you're going to pitch away from him. And that's what I was referring about pitchers watching guys hit in batting practice. The hitter will tell you what he can and cannot do. And I think pitchers are able to change better than a hitter can, because a hitter's got one speed.

He gets the bat through the strike zone and whatever. He can change the way he changes his feet and that sort of thing. But hitting is a talent, and I don't think it's something that can be cultivated as much other than ability. And, you know, I remember pitching against Joe DiMaggio in the All-Star Game, and with that wide spread he had hitting and where he held the bat, I felt like I could throw a fastball by him inside.

And he hit a double down the left field line in Ebbets Field. I didn't go back in there again either. But, yeah, hitters tell you the story and I think good hitters see the ball better than others, or maybe they pick up the rotation or whatever it is. And, you know, everybody I hear talk about hitting is that you don't look at the pitcher's motion, but you wait to see the ball and then hit it. And I think that's true.

And that's a discipline that a lot of guys don't have. And I think slumps are self-inflicted, that a guy starts worrying about the fact that he isn't hitting and he prolongs that slump. Well, the same thing could apply to pitching, too.

I think you get a little hitch in your motion or in your rhythm. Yeah, pitchers lose rhythm and you've got to find it. And when I was warming up to pitch a ball game, the first thing I would do is throw to get my arm loose, of course, and then feel; feel the release of the ball and where the ball went when I threw it and what kind of tools I had to pitch the ball game with.

You've got to get the first out before you can pitch the ball game. Then you've got to add the second out and the third out. And all of a sudden you're in trouble, and now you got the good hitters coming up. That's not the place to be. You've got to get that first guy out. Think of it this way. If I get the first three guys out in the first inning, now I make a leadoff hitter out of the fourth hitter, which wasn't what the manager intended. And you go four, five, six. Now, you've got the bottom end of the lineup coming in the third inning and that's all in your favor. But that little innocent base on balls or that pitch that you made a mistake with, they can come back and haunt you. And it's a funny thing. In the ninth inning, if you've struggled through the ball game, you always face those good hitters in the ninth inning.

When I first came to the big leagues I felt like I could throw pretty good. I was a high fastball pitcher. I threw a fastball, a curveball, and a change. And as the years went on I learned to pitch low in the strike zone. Lew Burdette used to say the best pitch in baseball is the one that looks like a strike and then isn't. And I think that stuck there, too. And you play with the ego of the hitter.

I think there are categories: There are pitchers; there are throwers; and freaks. And I don't want to be classified in any of those. I want to be able to think with the other manager. I want to be able to understand what he's going to do if so-and-so happens, and base on balls is a big part of it, that, you know, you want to eliminate situations before they happen.

I think the timing of the hitter's swing determines whether that groundball goes between first and second or at the second baseman or maybe at the first baseman. But good hitters seem to have that knack of hitting the ball in between the infielders or the outfielders. And that's the timing mechanism. And if you go a step further with that, when I was in a mode where I felt I could forecast what was going to happen, I would move the shortstop over toward second base when I know that hitter is going to hit it there.

And what a great feeling that is, when you know that you can make the hitter hit the ball where you want him to hit it. And that's when the game is fun. The tough part of the game is when you're out there struggling. And I think that happens with pitchers and hitters. And I also think the tough thing about hitting is that those guys are out there day after day after day and it's got to dwell on your thoughts when you've gone 0-for-12. Now, when is that first hit going to come?

And isn't it amazing too, that a guy can hit the ball off his fists and it falls in for a base hit and now he's out of his slump. But he can hit the ball hard twelve times and right at somebody. That's the wonderful thing about our game of baseball.

In the off-season I worked. I used to throw bales of hay around daily. I used to feed the cattle. I used to build fences, get my hands and face dirty.

And I remember management and coaches used to get mad at me because I used to throw the ball as hard the first day of spring training as I did when the season was over because God gave me that kind of an arm. And it just felt good to throw the ball hard.

Let me tell you something: I came up to the big leagues for $250 a month. Glad to get it. And I had to fight for every penny I ever got. And (General Manager) John Quinn wasn't the most generous guy in the world. And I remember (General Manager) John McHale, after I'd pitched twenty years in the big leagues, made a public statement that I'd earned a million dollars in my career. Well, guys look good in the lobby and get that as a signing bonus now.

Hey, look, one year I was holding out and Birdie Tebbetts was the manager. And he called me at home. And Birdie liked to think that he was a psychologist. And he said "Well, we're going to miss you." In other words, "Go ahead, stay home. We're not going to sign you."

And Birdie was the manager and I said, "How come you're intervening in place of the general manager in my negotiations?"

And he says, "Well, it's my ball club, you know." And, anyway, doesn't matter. But we had no bargaining power. We weren't allowed to have an agent.

Eighty-seven thousand five hundred dollars is the highest I made. I wanted $100,000. I couldn't get it. And, but then John Quinn, you know, I don't remember what he offered me, but he negotiated to split the difference with me. That's why that $87,500 was there.

In 1953 we went to spring training; the Boston Braves went out as the Milwaukee Braves. But I think an interesting story about that though is that Lou Perini, the owner, went to Notre Dame and one of his close friends there was Fred Miller, the owner of the Miller Brewing Company. And Fred Miller wanted Perini to take the Braves to Milwaukee, and they had just built a new stadium, et cetera, et cetera.

And to this day I think if Fred Miller had lived—he died in a plane crash—I think if he had lived, the Braves would still be in Milwaukee, and they'd be the Milwaukee Millers. But, you know, fate changes things so much. But at any rate, Miller was a great person for Milwaukee. Lou Perini was loved in Boston. So that when that change came about we were very surprised. And old beat-up, dilapidated Braves Field now became this brand-new ballpark in Milwaukee.

And then those people, the way they were, it was heaven-sent that, what a great place to play baseball. And, you know, we drew, like, 40,000 every game. The last year we were in Boston we drew 400,000 people. And the first year in Milwaukee we drew

1,800,000. And I remember I was holding out and I was talking to John Quinn about a raise. And he offered me a contract of my salary plus ten cents on every ticket after 400,000. I'd have been the highest paid player in baseball had I accepted that.

Well, I spent more time in Milwaukee than Boston; however, it was still the Braves. And, you know, I have a lot of fond memories of Boston. I was married there. My son was born there. Farber, Dr. Farber was a good friend of mine. You know, a lot of good memories in Boston. But I'm darn glad we went to Milwaukee, and I'm glad we won two pennants there, and I'm glad that we beat the damn Yankees.

Well, let me go back to '52, if I may. You know, after we lost the World Series in '48, the Braves went through a mode of rebuilding the ball club, and until '52 we were horrible. But that was the year that Eddie Mathews came up. That was the year that the nucleus of that ball club that went to Milwaukee was established.

Lew Burdette

And that was '52. Now '53: We got Joe Adcock; we had Billy Bruton, I think. And then in '54 Bobby Thomson broke his ankle in spring training. That afforded Hank Aaron to be brought up to the big league and he was only eighteen years old. And you know the great career he had. And so that, that ball club jelled and it was from, like, '53 to '57 when we finally won the pennant and beat the damn Dodgers and, you know, we were always in contention.

Oh, yeah. Oh, yeah, we played the Yankees in '57, and I always felt the World Series was a series that you played the Yankees. Cleveland, okay; that was a World Series, but it wasn't like playing the Yankees in the World Series. And then we beat them in '57. We beat them—well, Burdette pitched a great ball game in the seventh game of the World Series. And then in '58, we had the Yankees beat three games to one. And we blew it. We stopped hitting. And I think the worst part of that was the fact that our wives enjoyed the winner's cut of the World Series in '57. And then we had to take the loser's share in '58, and they had all that World Series money spent before we lost the Series. So it was double jeopardy. And you know, two great ball clubs played 14 games and each won 7. So I don't think that there was any differential as to who was better than who.

Eddie Mathews worked like a devil. In '52 he couldn't catch a groundball. And he must have taken 1,000 groundballs every day until he could do it. And then we had a hole at second base for a long time and then (Red) Schoendienst was available because he had trouble with his lungs. And we got him from the Giants, I believe. And he filled a great spot at second base. And I talked to Johnny Logan not long ago, and he said he learned more from Schoendienst playing with him than he ever did playing with any second baseman in baseball.

And, you know, the thing I liked about Red is that I'd be in trouble, Red would come to the mound and he said, "Make them hit the ball to me." And most times the infielders don't want any part of a crucial play. And then we had Adcock at first base. Great hitter. Great guess hitter. And was great on thrown balls, terrible with groundballs. I saw balls go between his body and his glove that went for base hits because he couldn't field worth a darn. You know, I think it was a mental block with him. And thrown balls, holy cow. He was so big and he could pick the ball out of the dirt with the best of them.

And then, in that Series we had Wes Covington in left field, who is a good left-handed hitter. Not too much defensively; you know, we kind of protected Adcock at first base and Covington in left field. So you try to make the hitter hit the ball to other places, but boy could he hit. And when you think of our lineup, you know, we had Bruton, who could run like a deer leading off. And then we had Schoendienst hitting second, and then Mathews, Aaron, Adcock. We had a potent lineup.

The Yankees? Well, first of all Mickey switch-hit, so that was an advantage. And from home to first, he could run as well as anybody. And I faced him when he was right-handed, and I always felt that Mickey had more power right-handed than he did left-handed. And I remember in one of the games, well, I think the day that I pitched a two-hitter, Mickey hit a ball that was inside the trademark, between his hands and the trademark.

And he hit it against the left center field fence at the scoreboard for a triple. And, you know, he was so strong that he didn't have to hit the ball well. And he hit the ball on the barrel most of the time. And, you know, he had a great kidlike atmosphere to him, enjoyed playing the game. And Yogi, they threw the mold away when they made Yogi.

You had to pitch carefully to Yogi. He could hit the ball over his head. I remember one time when I was with the Mets, Yogi was hitting as a pinch hitter. We were both coaches together then. And somebody threw him a curveball that bounced, like, four feet in front of the plate. And it bounced up and Yogi hit it for a home run. And when he came into the dugout I said, "Hey, Yogi, that's illegal."

He said, "What do you mean?"

And I said, "Well, the ball is dead when it hits the ground."

He said, "Not when it's in the strike zone." So this was Yogi's philosophy.

And I had good luck with Yogi. And I finally decided the best way to pitch Yogi is down the middle. Make him make up his mind about how he was going to hit it. You pitch him over his head, he'd hit a line drive somewhere. You pitch him a foot off the ground and he hit that for whatever.

Every time I pitched against the Yankees I was pitching against Whitey. And he was tough. And he moved the ball in and out. And did you ever notice how many times Whitey used to tie his shoelace during the game? Because Burdette taught him how to throw a mud ball. And he'd wet the ball and put it on the ground and it was a little heavier on one side than the other, and he'd make the ball move because of that.

Walt Moryn hit me pretty good and I decided, I'd been playing around with the spitter because of Burdette, and I played around with it in the bullpen. So I decided I was going to throw it to Moryn, and he hit it for a home run. And when he went around third base I said, "Hey, Walt, you hit my spitter."

He said, "It didn't spit." So that's the last time I ever tried to throw it.

Then I talked to Burdette about it and he says, "You got to have two wet fingers and a dry thumb." I remember him saying that so much. And then I was the pitching coach with Cleveland when Gaylord Perry was there. And Gaylord used to use Vaseline, and they were both good. Burdette threw a spitter to Tony Kubek in the World Series, and Tony was a high fastball hitter and that ball was up in his eyes.

And by the time the ball got to home plate it hit home plate. And Tony followed it with his hands and he swung and he broke the bat on home plate. That's how much that ball broke. But anyway, the Yankees had quality people in every position. They had a good bench. They had good starting and relief pitching. Yeah, they were a tough opponent.

I saw Henry Aaron when he first came up and, you know, I never saw the ball jump off somebody's bat like his. And Hank used to look like he was asleep between pitches. But when he saw that ball, everything went in motion.

Hank Aaron

I always felt that Hank had the ability to hit .400 because his power was in right center field. And all of a sudden he wanted to outdo Willie Mays and Eddie Mathews so he started pulling more and more and more. And as a result his batting average went down a little bit, but he started hitting home runs. And he is the greatest home run hitter in the history of baseball right now.

Hank was built—you know, the amazing thing about him: I think he had a waist of, like, twenty-eight inches. And, you know, Hank weighed about 175 pounds. But big hands, big wrists, big forearms, and I see all these people that are lifting weights in baseball today. You don't need those things. All you need is forearms and wrists. I think Ted Williams proved that. Musial proved that. And Hank.

And I thought, "This guy is special." Then we were playing St. Louis and it had rained before the game so that the ground was wet. And Hank was playing right field. And I think it was Marty Marion that hit the ball and hit it over Hank's head. And when he turned to run back, he slipped. And when he did, his glove hand went down to the ground and, you know, now his back is to the infield. And he threw up his right hand to catch his balance and the ball hit in it and he caught it.

And I thought, "God gave this guy the kind of ability that he's going to do great things in baseball." And he proved that right. But, you know, he wanted to steal more bases than Willie Mays, until he broke his ankle. Then the club wouldn't let him run anymore. He wanted to outdo Mathews in home runs, and he did that. I think Hank could have been a 20-game winner if he wanted to pitch. That's how good he was. And his endurance, his physique, he was a perfect ballplayer. If you had to clone ballplayers, he might be the one to clone.

Willie Mays got his first base hit off me. Willie Mays got his first home run off me. Same pitch. So I realized before the rest of the league that he was going to be a good hitter. And over the years I think Willie hit more home runs off me than anybody. Yeah, he was like a cobra at the plate, that he would uncoil. I saw him swinging at curveballs against a right-hander that he looked absolutely stupid. And yet, the ball he hit for a homer off me was a curveball. They didn't tell that it was from a right-hander instead of a left-hander.

You know, after a certain period there are goals you'd like to reach. And I think I'd like to reach for the moon and settle for whatever happens in the interim. And I feel that way about being the winningest left-hander. Number one, I worked cheap. God gave me a good arm. I loved playing baseball. I think I was afraid of that outside world, that I liked what I did for a living. And so, as a result, I happened to win 363 games. I'm proud of that. I guess I admired Carl Hubbell and Lefty Grove and those other people that were left-handed, but I happened to win more games than they did.

I dreaded the time that I was told I couldn't play anymore. And mind you, I was sold from the Braves in Milwaukee to the Mets, and my ego said I could win with the Mets as well as the Braves. When I got there I found out differently. We found a different way to lose every day when I was with the Mets. And I finished my career with San Francisco.

I didn't think I was a no-hitter pitcher. Then I happened to pitch two of them in my late career. And especially the one against the Giants, because boy, did they have some guys that could swing the bat. Mays, McCovey, Alou, oh, go down the line. They had a good ball club. And I was able to pitch a no-hitter against them, so I'm very proud of that one.

Well, you know, my name is synonymous with baseball, and I often wondered what I would have done with my life had I not played baseball. And Warren Spahn would have been somebody out there that nobody ever heard of if it hadn't been for baseball. That's the majesty of our game of baseball. I'd like to think that I was a role model for kids. I didn't have a drug addiction. I didn't dissipate in any way.

I was able to go out on the mound whenever my time came up. Good, bad, or indifferent, whatever I did in a game, and some of them weren't too good, it was my best that day. So that persever-ance and stick-to-it-iveness are the type of things you'd like to be proud of. I think that I'd like to be remembered for that.

I also would like to be remembered as a human being. That we have, you know, feelings and whatever like everybody else; so that we aren't clones that God put on earth just to play baseball, that baseball is played by human beings. And I think that's the exciting thing about it, is that you have personalities, human beings, and go out there and compete for nine innings. And there is no time clock; that the game is over when it's over. That's a Yogi-ism.

And as far as that, I am very proud of my baseball career. I'm very proud of my military career. And I have beautiful grandpeople and I have a great son that I'm very grateful for.

LARRY DOBY

The numbers are impressive enough—a seven-time All-Star outfielder, he led the AL twice in home runs, knocked in over 100 runs five times—but to fully understand the importance of Larry Doby's baseball life one has to look beyond mere statistics.

At a time when African-Americans were routinely segregated not only in baseball but in life, Doby displayed his talent when he finally got the chance to perform in the big leagues as the AL's first black player.

After playing four seasons with Newark of the Negro National League, Doby made his major league debut on July 5, 1947, for the Cleveland Indians, just eleven weeks after Jackie Robinson broke the color barrier with the Brooklyn Dodgers. A year later he helped Cleveland win the 1948 World Series against the Boston Braves, batting .318 in the Fall Classic and hitting the winning home run in Game 5. Doby was also a major contributor in 1954 when the Indians won a record 111 games, finishing second in the AL MVP voting after leading the league with 32 home runs and 126 RBI.

"He certainly endured a great deal of prejudice, and Larry handled it as well as anybody could handle it," said Cleveland teammate Al Rosen. "He was a tough, hard-nosed player. It was very difficult for him. There's no doubt about that. He was just an outstanding player and a terrific teammate."

Throughout his career Doby was also breaking down racial barriers, whether it was becoming the first black player to hit a home run in the

World Series, win a home run title in the majors, or win an RBI title in the AL.

"He was kind of like Buzz Aldrin, the second man on the moon, because he was the second African-American player in the majors behind Jackie Robinson," said Cleveland teammate and fellow Hall of Famer Bob Feller. "He was just as good a ballplayer, an exciting player, and a very good teammate. He helped us win the World Series in 1948. He was a great ballplayer, a great American, and an excellent teammate."

WELL, I REMEMBER VIVIDLY where I was involved in baseball when I was like nine, ten years old. We had a fellow in the town by the name of Richard DuBose, who had a Model T Ford. And he used to gather the kids together, and we'd play different teams around the city. And my father had played semipro ball with the team that Richard DuBose played for.

I've always said that I think the toughest things for some of my teammates when I first got to Major League Baseball was the fact that they had not had the opportunity to associate with Afro-American people.

I lost my father when I was about eight years old. And my mom was in the North because at that particular time, the salary was a little different in the North than in the South. So I grew up—I was raised by an aunt and an uncle and a grandmother. And I think that, the one thing that my grandmother taught me is a respect for people as human beings.

Judge people on your own, not on what somebody else may tell you or what you might read. She was very strict from the standpoint of believing in a Supreme Being. I always say that a lot of the things that happened to me in the early stages of baseball, that I was able to adjust to or controlled to a certain extent, is there was a strong feeling that God above was the reason why you did not get yourself involved in things that you could have.

The person that helped me most in Camden (South Carolina)

Larry Doby

was a fellow by the name of Richard DuBose that I mentioned before. My father passed when I was eight years old, so I never got a chance to really remember too much about my father as far as helping me playing the game of baseball. But the fellow that, that lived in the town that had these kids come together to play baseball taught me a lot. And then when I got to high school in Paterson, New Jersey, I had a coach by the name of Al Livingston who helped me a lot. I played semipro ball in Paterson, and a fellow by the name of Pat Wilson was involved, and he helped me a lot.

I came north when I went to high school—my first year in high school. In Camden, I went to a missionary school. And when I finished grade school, I came north, and lived with my mom. The segregation part was the same. There wasn't any difference. You know, you had segregation in the South and you had segregation in the North; it wasn't any different.

But one of the interesting things about the segregation in the North and those in the South is that being on these different high school teams, on a Saturday, you'll get together with the football team or the baseball team or the basketball team, and you all go to the movies. And we all walked, because you didn't have money for a bus or your parents didn't have a car.

So what would happen when we walked to the movies, and we all lived in a mixed neighborhood in Paterson, is that they would go downstairs and I would go upstairs. Well, at that particular time, Afro-Americans couldn't sit downstairs in movies. But the important thing is that we all walked together, and we all walked back home together.

You know, one of the things, and I think at the time that I was involved in the early stages of games in baseball, I didn't realize what the history would be. I knew things that I couldn't do. Bill Veeck, who when I walked into his office, he had a scrapbook about that high, and from the day I was born until I walked in that office, with what I had done. And one of the things that I think that—I know really helped, besides believing in a Supreme Being, is that he said to me, "You know, we're in this together."

And then he started mentioning the fact, the importance as far as the history is concerned. I had no knowledge of what the history was at that particular time. But my thing was, I wanted to play baseball. And at the time, I never thought that I would get the opportunity. I thought I'd get the opportunity when Jackie signed in 1945 for Montreal. I was on an island called Ulithi in the South Pacific. And there were two Major League Baseball players on the island with me, one named Mickey Vernon, and the other was a fellow by the name of Billy Goodman.

So they knew that I had played in the Negro Leagues. And we used to go out on the island and throw batting practice at each other. And, a matter of fact, Mickey Vernon turned my name in to Mr. Griffith at the time, but at that time, Washington wasn't ready for an Afro-American ballplayer.

I had not too much knowledge of major league players at that particular time because I never went to a ball game. My family couldn't afford a radio to listen. So there were people in my school that I wanted to be like.

And one fellow went to my high school, named Bob Smith—Afro-American, great athlete. And, you know, that's the kind of person that I wanted to be like. When I got to the Newark Eagles, you know, playing against Josh (Gibson) and Satch (Paige) and those guys, then all the sudden you kind of want to be like those guys. And a lot of people say, "Well, you never had a major league player as a hero?" No, I didn't, because I never went to a game and—I used to sell newspapers, and I used to read about these different players, you know. But I never wanted to be like those players because there wasn't anybody representing Afro-Americans in Major League Baseball.

I graduated high school in 1942—June 1942. And the Newark Eagles was playing in my hometown, playing a team called the Black Yankees. There was an umpire in the Negro Leagues was from my hometown. And he suggested to Abe and Effa Manley, who owned the Eagles, to give me a tryout.

So I went for a tryout and I made the team. And they gave me $300 a month. I was seventeen.

But when you went around the league, you knew who could play. The Monte Irvins and the Lenny Pearsons, those guys were the big guys. And then all of a sudden here comes this little guy out of high school. And by playing well, I began to have a fan following. You know, I'll tell you that I had a real good time playing in the Negro Leagues.

Even before some of us got the opportunity to play in Major League Baseball, we had played in stadiums like Yankee Stadium and the Polo Grounds and Ebbets Field and Comiskey Park and Griffith Stadium. And what they would have is, they called it a two-team doubleheader. When the Yanks are out of town we would play in Yankee Stadium. And you'd play the Newark Eagles against the Baltimore Elite Giants. And you'd have people like Monte Irvin, myself, Roy Campanella, Joe Black, Junior Gilliam.

And then the second game would be the Monarchs against the Philadelphia Stars. And the Monarchs would have Satchel Paige, and a fellow by the name of Hank Thompson, and then another fellow by the name of Harry Simpson, all got major league situations. And then the Homestead Grays would play the Newark Eagles. You'd have Josh Gibson and Buck Leonard and Cool Papa Bell. And you'd have like 40,000, 45,000 people. That's why sometimes I think, and I think a lot of people think the same way, that Mr. Rickey saw more than just players.

And that's business, you know. If you get 40,000 Afro-Americans in the stadium, that's, even if it's only a dollar a head, that's $40,000. But, the thing that was interesting is that the dress, the shirt, the tie, and the hat. And most of the Afro-Americans that was at the ballpark just came from church. And, they go to church at 11:00, the game started at 1:00, so they're in the ballpark.

And, if you look at some of the old clippings of people in the major leagues, they're all dressed nice. And nothing against people today the way they're dressed, that's fine. But that was a part of the so-called luxury thing for Afro-Americans at that particular time, because you go to church, and then you come to the ballpark, and it, you know, it didn't cost a lot of money. And you would enjoy, seeing these different people play.

I think that Afro-Americans, as far as the Negro Leagues were concerned, were great contributors to the Negro League Baseball, because they were great supporters. And great rooters, they root for you like mad. And I remember in 1946 when the Newark Eagles won the Negro World Series, and we beat Satchel Paige two games, 3-to-2 and 2-to-1.

And what they would do is, they would have the game, one game in Newark, they'd have another game in New York, they'd have another game in Philadelphia, and they'd have another game in Washington. By going around to different cities, they would draw more people. And one of the things that was so great about it was that Satch was sort of a promoter, or market man, or whatever you want to call it.

And he would fill the stadium. And he was the kind of a guy

that would say, "Well, I'm gonna throw you a fastball," you know, and he'd throw you the fastball. People talk about the pitching aspect, in particular, Satchel Paige. You got to stay low or you stay high. Satch just stayed low all the time, just threw the ball low. Satch, if you have seen Pedro Martinez, same kind of a movement on the pitch. And finger-wise. If you notice how long Pedro's fingers are, Satchel's fingers were long like that and a thin hand, and just a nice easy, easy movement.

There was no such thing as jealousy, or no such thing as not being together as a team, not only on the baseball field, but off the baseball field. And I think that's one of the things that I miss tremendously about when I first got involved with baseball. Because even in high school, when you play a game and the game is over, you go to a soda fountain. And you sit down and talk and have a soda. When I was in the Negro Leagues, the same thing. You went with the team—with the players when the game was over. There's not much of a drinking aspect.

Well, when in '46, when we won the World Series, I was making $700 a month. Because I had come out of the service, so they raised me from $300 to $700. Now, when you play at the World Series, we each got $1,500 extra. So you're talking about a pretty good amount of money coming—when you talk about being twenty, twenty-one years old, and you're making that kind of money, you never, you never thought that you would be in that position to make that kind of money.

One thing that bothered me a little bit when I first went into the service is, I got on the train in Newark, New Jersey—I was in the Navy, going to Great Lakes Naval Station, Illinois, and there was a lot of athletes that I played with and played against; we were all on the same train. So I'm thinking that we're all going to be together. Well, you didn't know the history of the service as far as integration is concerned.

You just thought, you just thought when you go into the service to fight, everybody's going to be together. Anyway, when we get to Great Lakes, and into boot camp—my camp was a camp called

Robert Small. It was separated from the main camp where the Caucasian kids lived. So when we got off the train, I'm thinking we are going to go together. No, I went that way, and they went that way. And the only time I saw those kids would be when they have a game.

There would be a football game, a baseball game. That kind of hurt a little bit because, if you had gone to school with people you'd been around these kids for four years, you don't have a chance to think about segregation, because you're all playing the game together; a lot of us lived in the same neighborhood. You walk home together. You go to school together. And then when you get into that situation, there's a difference as far as being with these kids that you grew up with.

The other part that was disappointing is they had football, baseball, and basketball teams, but they weren't integrated. You had the Great Lakes Negro baseball team, Great Lakes Negro basketball team. The football team was integrated, because Paul Brown was the coach. And he had guys like Marion Motley and those guys playing for him. And, most of the guys he had—well all the guys he had on the Great Lakes baseball team were from college.

This was the first time that segregation really stung me like this. I wasn't expecting it in the military. I had no idea. It hurt a lot. It hurt as much as when I walked into Cleveland; I had to stay in a different hotel in Chicago or a different hotel in, in St. Louis. But I had been able to adjust to that much easier, because I had adjusted to the Army situation. Now, coming out of high school, and going into the Army, it was a little bit harder to adjust than it was coming out of the service, going into baseball.

I was on a basketball team, all-Afro-American basketball team. And I was on a baseball team, all-Afro-American baseball team. And we'd travel around Chicago playing different semipro teams, played the House of David and a lot of the local teams, semipro teams around there.

And then I got promoted to a specialist A, and I went to Treasure Island, San Francisco, stayed a couple of months as a trainer.

And then I went to Guam and stayed a couple months. And then I wound up on a little island in the South Pacific called Ulithi. And I was a physical ed trainer on that island. And that's when I met Mickey Vernon of the Washington Senators and Billy Goodman of the Boston Red Sox.

We would go out and throw for each other. And when I came back to Paterson, when I got discharged in January of 1946, I went to San Juan, Puerto Rico, played winter ball. And I wrote Mickey Vernon a letter, and I said, "I'd like to, to have a couple of your bats."

And he sent me a dozen Louisville Sluggers. Mickey Vernon bat, Louisville Sluggers, the first major league bat that I had ever had.

I got out January of '46, played in Puerto Rico that winter, and then came back to go to spring training with the Newark Eagles in Jacksonville, Florida. That 1946 Newark Eagle baseball team was one of the best teams I've played on. It reminds me a lot of the 1948 Cleveland Indians baseball team.

I think four guys from that Negro League team are in the Hall of Fame: Monte Irvin, myself, Leon Day, and a shortstop by the name of Willie Wells, who was my manager when I got there—great player, and Ray Dandridge, of course, another great player.

The first time I heard about anybody talking to me about Major League Baseball was like in May of '47. Lou Jones came to my house in Paterson, and went to a game with me in Trenton, New Jersey—we were playing the Giants.

And coming back with him from Trenton, he mentioned the fact that I had been scouted by a fellow by the name of Bill Killapher, who was the head scout with the Indians. And the question he asked me, "Do you think you can play Major League Baseball?" And you know you're thinking that you can play baseball. Yeah. I can play baseball, you know. And, you know, the emphasis as far as Major League Baseball was concerned didn't concern me.

I went on and kept playing with Newark. So July 4, we had a doubleheader against the Philadelphia Stars, and he came that morning. And he said, "We're going to take a train back to Chicago after the game is over." So I played the first game—matter of fact I

Bill Veeck

hit a home run. And my teammates gave me a kit, you know, going away. And we got on the train I think like six o'clock in the afternoon in Newark, got into Chicago the next morning. Bill Veeck was in the hotel in his office. And Lou Jones took me to him to sign a contract.

And that's when Mr. Veeck said to me, "This is a history type thing going on and, you know, there are things that you can't do. You know, if you do them, it might change the whole picture as far as integrating baseball is concerned for Afro-Americans."

It's a kind of a feeling that you can't believe it. You know you really can't believe it. I mean, you've signed the contract. You're going to play Major League Baseball, but you really can't believe it. The time that I really believed it is when I put the uniform on and my first time at bat when I would pinch-hit. And then the second time when I played the second game. Then I know I'm in the major leagues.

Never thinking that I'm not going to be able to make it, you know, that never crossed my mind. People say, "Well, did you ever have any doubts?" I never had any doubts.

The minute I signed the contract in Veeck's office, Lou Jones, who was the public relations man—matter of fact, he was Lena Horne's first husband—he brought me to Lou Boudreau, the manager. And then Boudreau had the players lined up. I was going right on the roster, no minor leagues.

Boudreau [Indians manager Lou Boudreau] had me pinch hit and I struck out. The second game I played first baseman and I got a double and drove in a run. Now, that's the only full game I played in 1947. The rest of it was pinch-hitting here and there. I was used to being up four times and getting the four whacks at it. I didn't know the pitchers, but even if you didn't know the pitchers, when you play a full game, you still know you've got four chances. And if you've got one chance, it's a little bit more difficult, you know, because when you go up to pinch-hit and you fail, it lingers on your mind longer than if you go 0-for-4.

I think the most important part of that meeting in Mr. Veeck's office was when he said to me that we're in this together. You can look in a person's eye and tell a lot about their sincerity although I didn't know him until I got into baseball. But he was the kind of a person—after I got into baseball I learned that was a person that believed in human beings and sort of rooted for the underdog.

And if you say underdog at that particular time, I think most Afro-Americans were considered underdogs. So when he made that statement to me, I relaxed. It made me relax a lot.

When he said that we're in this together and then he went into the fact that this is a historical thing, which I had not thought too much about. The other thing is that you're going to have a lot of people that are not going to agree with what we're doing. If the umpire should happen to call a pitch that you think may be a ball or a strike, you can't turn around and, question it. If you slide into second base and someone happens to rough you up a little bit, you've got to get up and walk away.

There was one person on the ball club that he mentioned to me that I could go to and that was a fellow by the name of Bill McKechnie, who was the coach at the time. He was very instrumental in the change that came about from second base to the outfield. The other person that automatically came up and welcomed me was a fellow by the name of Jim Hegan, and the other fellow—my good friend just passed away, Bob Lemon. And Joe Gordon. Those four people were very kind to me, very good.

He (Veeck) said some of these guys are not going to welcome you like you think you should be welcomed. He says you're going to have a lot of guys that don't want you here. And he says the one thing you'd have to worry about I know who they are, and they won't be here next year. So as I went down the line, of course, those guys—they showed up. The most hurting part of that whole situation was when Boudreau said to me you're playing first base the second game, and I didn't have a first baseman's glove.

I had never played first base before. And I had a second baseman's glove. And a person on the team wouldn't let me have his glove. So they had to go to the White Sox and borrow a glove for me, you know, to play first base. That bothered me a little bit.

Hegan just shook my hand and said, "Good luck," and Lemm said—Lemm used to always use the word "meat." He said, "Good luck, meat," you know.

Of the players on other teams, Dominic DiMaggio said to me, congratulations. Ted Williams said to me, congratulations. And there was a fellow that played first base for the Red Sox at that time [1947], named Rudy York; he was one of the other people. Now, I'm talking about in '48 when I was playing [Fenway], because you know at that time, you left your glove on the field, so that when you go by DiMaggio or you go by Williams there, it's there.

On that first day in my Cleveland uniform I was very disappointed for five or ten minutes because, you know, even in high school, you warm up with somebody, and you have a good time because, you've been doing this for a long time. Then you go to

Negro Leagues, warm up with a person, you've been doing that for a long time. Then you go into the major leagues and you walk out on the field and you're standing there for five or ten minutes before somebody will warm up with you, and a fellow by the name of Joe Gordon warmed up with me that day and did it the rest of the year. He said, "Come on, kid," and we started warming up together.

Gordon definitely sent a message because Gordon was very well thought of, and if you play for the Yankees, you're the best—you know, I don't care. You know, you're just great. You could be mediocre and play for the Yankees, and that'd make you a star. But Joe wasn't mediocre. So for Gordon to come forward like that, and particularly coming from the Yankees, it meant a lot to me and it taught those other people something as far as a relationship is concerned.

The crowd in Chicago, they were very quiet. There wasn't a lot of noise or rumbling being made about that situation, although the history was made in Chicago. There were not that many Afro-Americans in the ballpark at that time.

I come home for the winter in '47, and I went to work in the post office, where I had done before. And worked out during the winter, worked out at the YMCA during the winter. And went to spring training in '48, and that's when stuff started happening.

I had contact with Jackie Robinson only once that summer of '47. They had a thing they called the Knothole Gang, and we'd play an exhibition game in Cleveland and one in Brooklyn, and all the proceeds would go to the charity, and that's when he and I would talk a little bit. You know, a funny thing. All those years I would meet him or I would see him someplace or he'd see me someplace, the only thing that we talked about is the person on the other ball club. You know, at that time, you had a lot of bench jockeys. Person who "owned" the ball club, that would be the kind of person that you had to watch out for. I would tell him the people in the American League, and he'd tell me the people in the National League.

One of the things that he knew and I knew—we were both going through the same type thing. You know, sometimes when people say, well, the first, you know, which is true as far as Jack's

Jackie Robinson

being the first is concerned and having the problems with the people with—you know, you get the threatening letters, "We're going to shoot you," or you get some guy in the stand that'll say, "Well, who was your wife out with last night?"

Or the name-calling—it's a funny thing. I laugh now. It wasn't funny at the time but the "N" word—I was called the "N" word so much that it got to the point where, I didn't hear it. I mean, you hear it, but it didn't bother you like the first time. Like in '48, you're going to St. Louis, and somebody yelled the "N" word, and then you come to New York, you go to Washington, and all of a sudden, after about three or four years, you heard it so much until it just disappeared.

We were in St. Louis, which was a bad town for me, and this

loudmouth came down the aisle, and he said to me, "I wonder who your wife was out with last night."

And I just dropped the bat, and I started into the stands, and Bill McKechnie grabbed me by the belt and pulled me back. He said, "You can't go up in those stands." You know, you lose your thinking as to what you could not do and what your purpose is for being there because I think when someone talks about your wife or your mom, it's a little different than somebody calling you, using the "N" word, you know?

You couldn't stay in the same hotels with your teammates, and you couldn't eat in the same restaurant. So on the road you were all alone. And one of the things that made it a little bit difficult with me is that you had too much time to think about the bad day you had. If you had somebody with you, you'd probably be talking about something else. But to have a bad day and to go back to the hotel by yourself with no one to talk to made it a little bit difficult as far as trying to forget about it. Now, you had to forget about it, but if I went 0-for-4 and went back to the hotel, I didn't forget about it right away.

Everywhere but New York, but I could stay in Paterson when I came to New York. St. Louis, Chicago, Washington, D.C., I could stay. But what they did was they changed the hotel. In Washington, the hotel, the Statler, was where they stayed before I got there. When I got there, they went to the Sheraton. Now, the Sheraton Hotel was where all the foreigners came in, you know, from Africa, from Nigeria, from Egypt. So as far as the mixture of people is concerned, you know, color-wise, they didn't know whether I was from Africa or whether I was from Egypt.

The Philadelphia Athletics had an AAA Club in Toronto. And Bill Veeck had worked an agreement with Mr. Connie Mack for me to go to Toronto in '48. Took me to spring training in '48, changed my position from second base to the outfield. And I had a good spring. And I made the club.

Nineteen forty-eight, September, Satchel Paige came. Veeck and Abe Saperstein (founder of the Harlem Globetrotters) were very close, and Saperstein asked Veeck to look at Satch. And Veeck was

Satchel Paige

a great promoter and Satch was an ideal person for him to promote, so—

Yeah, the problem with Satch was the hotels that we could stay
in, Satch wouldn't stay in them because, he'd been—all those hotels, particularly Afro-American hotels, he'd stayed in them long
before we did.

So he knew all these people, and instead of going to the Ken-
more in Boston, he'd go to the Afro-American hotel. And Boudreau
had a tough time dealing with that because he thought that if we
were allowed to stay in the hotel with the team, that we should. But
Satch would stay in the hotels that he'd stayed in before, so that's
one of the reasons why Satch only stayed with us a year or two and
then went to St. Louis.

Supposedly I roomed with Satch while he was with Cleveland, but I roomed with his luggage. Satch was—he was quite a character. I'll tell you, when we talk about promoting yourself, he's the first one that I realized how important it was, promoted himself, because he could do that very well. Well, he'd done that all his life, like he owned an airplane before he came to Cleveland, and he owned a chauffeur-driven Cadillac. See, what he would do is he'd pitch three innings in Newark in the Negro Leagues, and make himself a thousand dollars, okay? Like one o'clock game, three o'clock game in Philadelphia, make another thousand dollars, a night game in Washington, make another thousand dollars. Now, you're talking about $3,000 in one day, which is a lot of money— not every day, but which is a lot of money. And that's why he could afford a chauffeur-driven Cadillac and an airplane.

He was that good. I say that because I faced Satch when—I don't know what age it was, but he wasn't—wasn't a thirty-year-old man. And I've said to a lot of people that, from a pitching standpoint, I didn't face anybody better. Threw hard and great control, no question about it. And the easy motion and that kind of thing, and he would talk a lot about—some of the stuff I saw in a movie, where he was drinking on the mound, I don't never recall that. That wasn't true. But he did talk. He did say, "I'm going to throw you a fastball." No, he said, "Where do you want it? Fastball where? Down the middle?" He says, "I'll throw you a fastball down the middle." And the story about him calling the outfield in, that's a true story.

If someone would ask him, "Satch, how old are you?" he'd say, "Well, how old do you think I am?" Well, the person might say, "You're about forty." He'd say, "I'm forty." Someone else would say, "Well, you're about forty-five, fifty." He'd say, "I'm forty-five, fifty." Whatever number you threw out, that's what you would get. Veeck tried to get his birth certificate. He was born in Alabama somewhere. I forgot now where. But, you know, at that time, they weren't keeping birth certificates.

You know his hesitation pitch. He would start one up and drop the foot and then throw a ball. They took it out. He couldn't do it in the major league because they said it would distract the hitter, whatever the situation would be.

The guy I had trouble hitting in '48 was Allie Reynolds. High fastball, moving fastball up, and you know it's a funny thing, he used to get me out and laugh, he'd smile, you know. So, I said to him, one day, I said, "You're going to get old." And, sure enough he got old, I caught up with him.

I had good success against Eddie Lopat. I had good success against Whitey Ford, but Reynolds was the guy that was tough on me. I think one of the things that helped me as far as left-handers and right-handers is because I played every day against all pitchers. So, I was adjusted to them. There were some pretty good left-handers in the Negro Leagues that I played against.

In '48 I batted second for a while. And, then in '49 Boudreau put me in the number three spot, and I stayed in the number three

Allie Reynolds

spot the whole time that—even when I got traded to Chicago. When we start saying how they looked at me after they found that I could play, I think a lot of them looked at me not only as a person that had athletic ability and that could play, but as a person who was a human being like they were.

The color didn't make a difference as far as attitude, personality, and character, and all that, it just—the thing that I had that a lot of people have. So, the one thing that I think that I always say athletics can bring people closer together than most things is that you can judge as to whether you can depend on a person to do certain—in baseball, you depend on each other, and it has nothing to do with nationality.

You see I've always thought that one of the toughest things for me in baseball when I first got there was that I had to—strike out and walk back calmly; that is not the true me, all right. I want to kick things; I want to do everything.

But I couldn't let it go, not in '48. I did it in '54, '55, I began to kick water coolers, and, but, it was just the thing, now people just took for granted as part of the game.

The one thing about the World Series in '48, and I can say this and say it truthfully, I've always been treated very, very good by Cleveland fans. I cannot say one moment that I was mistreated by Cleveland fans. They were always good to me.

In the beginning they were kind of quiet, but as the years went on, I would get standing ovations like anybody else as far as the ball club was concerned. So, that, the other thing about Cleveland is that if we go back and look at the history and Cleveland was one of the ten cities in the United States that had showed progress as far as integration is concerned. You see, in '46 before I got there, you had a Marion Motley and a Bill Willis and an Horace Gillom playing football for the Cleveland Browns.

And then way back in '36 you had that guy that won the Olympics, Jesse Owens. So, you had the makings of me coming to Cleveland because you've had Afro-Americans involved in athletics in the town before that. So, I think that's one thing that helped me a lot to be welcomed more by the fans than I was by some of the people that I played with.

When I hit that home run that won Game 4 in the '48 World Series, there was a fellow by the name of Steve Gromek. He pitched and I hit the home run to win the game, and we embraced each other. And it wasn't an embrace where it was orchestrated or planned, it was just two happy people; and if you look at the smile of the two people, there was no such thing as a planned thing, or there's no such thing as a Hollywood thing; it's a thing of a joy of a happy moment in our lives that we had been able to accomplish.

Later, he was having some problems in his town about why are you hugging that so-and-so, and so his minister, he told me that his

Larry Doby and Steve Gromek

minister said to him that he would have done more than that if I'd hit a home run for him for the ball game. And, I thought that was a nice gesture. That was one of the great moments of my career. Now, you know, first of all, you have to say signing the contract, but the contract was something different from being in the World Series and hitting the home run to win the game. Certainly by signing the contract puts you in that position. But you don't think about the contract like you think about that particular moment in your life as far as hitting the home run.

I never thought of myself as—I know I represent a race, but I never put myself in a position to think "race." You see, for me, I was brought up thinking people; certainly I know I'm Afro-American descent, I know that, but my parents never taught me in terms of identification in terms of thinking about a special thing like a race.

The Negro League players helped change the nature of the way the game was played. Number one I think the change that came about is that— it's been a proven fact that you can play baseball. I mean, when people say, well, certainly, you were a success through the Negro League, but you can't be a success in the major leagues; that's been proven not to be true.

The other thing is important maybe before proven is that you got the opportunity to prove it. It also proves that opportunities are supposed to be given to every person who qualifies or who has the ability. Baseball being the all-American game certainly became the all-American game in 1947. You couldn't say baseball was the all-American game before 1947.

I'm not too sure that this is based on the social aspects, as far as the National League moving ahead of the American League as far as Afro-Americans are concerned, but I think it does have some effects as far as the truism is concerned that the American League may have been somewhat slow because the Yanks were winning all—most of the pennants. The All-Star Game was being won by the American League mostly, so that means that, in my opinion, that means that maybe the slowness as far as African-Americans were concerned was not needed as much as it was in the National League.

I think Jack (Robinson) brought a difference where speed's concerned, stealing bases, and I think that if you look at the American League, the American League is based on power mostly.

On my ball club nobody ran; you know, we had Gordon, we had Boudreau and those kind of guys, and then the Yanks had Rizzuto, a few guys, but there was mostly power. So, when these guys came to the National League, they changed the whole aspect as far as just stealing bases or quickness is concerned.

I think Jack had a lot to do with that, because he'd steal bases or steal home and that kind of situation. And, one of the things about the game of baseball I think that brings a certain amount of color to it is when a guy steals the base.

The one thing that I know is, the version of the Bible that says, "God put no more on you than you can bear." That's a true statement, and the way I feel about it. Because if you look at the situation that both of us, Mr. Robinson and myself, got involved in, you know, he put as much on you as you can bear. And, we bore all those negative things that we had to bear, and came out successfully.

I had the opportunity; it came; I took advantage of it. But the most important thing, I was prepared. I think being prepared is most important; because if you're not, you don't know when the opportunities are going to come.

RALPH KINER

For a period from the mid-1940s to the early 1950s, Ralph Kiner was a slugger without peer. Though his career would last only a decade, he is still remembered as one of the most powerful right-handed hitters the game has seen.

If it's true, as Kiner is reported to have said, that home run hitters drive Cadillacs while singles hitters drive Fords, then he must have had expensive taste in automobiles. The young outfielder relayed this theory in a 1949 magazine article: "My ambition ever since I came to the majors in 1946 has been to set a new home run record, or come mighty close to it. I would much prefer to hit 50 home runs in a season and bat .275 than hit 25 home runs and finish with .325."

Kiner hit 369 home runs during his ten-year career (1946–55), winning or sharing the National League crown in each of his first seven seasons. Kiner's power left former Pirates teammate Eddie Bockman in awe. "I was only a teammate of Ralph's for two years [1948–49], but I got to see 94 of his home runs. It seemed each one was hit farther than the last one. The thrills, the excitement, and the big part they played in each game will be something I will always remember."

Clyde McCullough, who saw Kiner as both a teammate and a foe, wonders what the slugger could have done in a more hitter-friendly park. "If he had played half a season in New York, or better still in Brooklyn, think how many he would have hit. He played in a tremendously big park in Pittsburgh [Forbes Field], even when they created Kiner's Korner, and

Ralph Kiner

in another big one in Cleveland. And when the wind blew in off the lake in Chicago, Wrigley Field was tough, too."

Bill Burwell, who had seen thousands of players as a major league player, coach, and manager, was also impressed after serving on the Pirates' bench during Kiner's heyday: "I've seen a lot of long-ball hitters in my day, but this kid has power that is honestly amazing. The balls fairly fly off his bat."

I WAS BORN IN 1922 and have no recollection of my father, who died when I was four and a half years old. And oddly enough, he died of a mastoid infection, which, of course, today would be nothing. It'd be cured in a short time. My mother then moved to California. She had a friend that lived in a town called Alhambra.

At the age of five, I was living there and was raised in that area. Fortunately for me, it was a neighborhood town. It was kind of a bedroom town of L.A., Los Angeles. We had vacant lots and what have you, and I had neighbors that had one son that was maybe, let's see, it would be five years older than I.

I used to go out and shag balls while his father pitched to him and he would hit. And along about, I guess, about a month of shagging balls for this kid, I said, "I'm going to quit, unless you let me hit."

So they said, "Okay. It's your turn now." That's really how I got started to play baseball.

That was at a very early age. I would've been about nine years old, or ten. In the grammar schools in California, we had a lot of softball games. I played an awful lot of fast-pitch softball and that was really the basis of my playing. But at the same time, I still played hardball, or regular baseball.

That was when Major League Baseball really meant something to me. Then, in 1934, the Cardinals and Detroit were in the World Series. I was in grammar school at that time and I was in a room in grammar school where I could look out the window and see a very close neighbor of mine. This lady's husband worked and she was the only one home. These were all day games.

She would come out on the porch and she'd whistle. Now, this whistle had to be a pretty good whistle, because I was at least 150, 200 yards away from where she was. She had a system devised so that she could signal me who was winning the game that was being played that day. And they didn't have the game on in the schoolroom, but it was on radio for her. So I'd just keep looking out there and she'd come out, and then she'd give me the signs who was ahead. So that was my really first following of Major League Baseball.

Why I took the Detroit Tigers, I have no idea, but that was my team. The Cardinals were an extremely colorful team at that time.

They had the Gashouse Gang, they had Dizzy Dean, they had Pepper Martin, and they had Frankie Frisch. It was really a colorful team. Pepper Martin was at third base. And I, for some reason, went for Detroit. I have no recollection of why it was that way, except they had one of the great hitters of all time in Hank Greenberg, and also the great second baseman Charlie Gehringer. And they had Mickey Cochrane. It was a colorful team too, and it was a great series. The Cardinals won in the seventh game when Dean pitched a shutout. They won by twelve—I think it was an 11–0 score. That was the game where they took Medwick, St. Louis Cardinals left fielder, out of the game. He had slid hard in the third base against Marvin Owen, and Owen and he got in a fight.

And then he went out to left field to take his position and the fans in left field bombarded him with whatever, apples, oranges, whatever, eggs, whatever they had. Landis stopped the game and took him out of the game. That was Kenesaw Mountain Landis, who was the commissioner of baseball.

So that was my association with the Tigers. Later on, I played with them in 1947, when Hank Greenberg came over to the Pirates. That was the first time I ever met him. He was really my idol and he proved to be the most important factor in my baseball life, later on.

At the age of maybe thirteen or fourteen, I was playing on a Sunday team with all men. I was able to play right field. I was the worst player on the team, but I was still young. They would let me play. I was good enough to play and help them with their winning games. That really got me into playing my first games of organized baseball.

It was all sandlot and pickup, and they had people that were adults playing on the team. And then, I went to high school and in the Alhambra High School, I made the varsity team. You couldn't play in your freshman year. I made it in my sophomore year and continued to play baseball. I guess, over the course of one year, I would play kind of the pickup games on the sandlots and the high school games and the American Legion games and the Sunday games and the Saturday games.

Ironically, I was picked up by a scout named Dan Crowley, who played in the Pacific Coast League baseball, which was the highest minor league at that time. He was the man that ran the Yankee Juniors. The Yankee Juniors were a team sponsored by the New York Yankees. We used to get the hand-down uniforms of the Yankee players that played in the majors.

Of course, the Yankees in those days—and we're talking about the '30s and '40s—were a dominating force. The great players were Babe Ruth and Lou Gehrig and what-have-you. It was quite a thrill to wear an old Yankee uniform. I never got Ruth's uniform, or Gehrig's, but I did get Selkirk's uniform, which I treasured like any kid would, when he had it.

I played for the Yankee Juniors for, I guess, three years. I was all set. They had an unwritten rule that if you played with these teams, you would be signed when you got to be of age, or out of high school, by that team. There was a scout named Hollis Thurston that scouted for the Pittsburgh Pirates who watched me play.

Thurston stole me away from the Yankees and I also had another good friend that was helping me with his son, who was my age, to play baseball, and he more or less handled my deal. His name was Harry Johnston. And he (Thurston) went to Mr. Johnston and said, "Look, if he signs with the Yankees, he's going to be in the minor leagues seven years," which was the case in those days.

So I was offered a bonus of $3,000 to sign with the Pirates. And the Yankees offered me a scholarship to USC, University of Southern California, and I debated which way to go.

And he (Thurston) convinced me that I —oh, they also would give me a contract in A-ball, which, at that time, was a third highest league, which would definitely shorten my time to get to the major leagues if I could play. So that was the inducement. And they also said they would give me $5,000 "if you make the major leagues," which was illegal. You couldn't have anything that wasn't written down and it was a verbal contract.

Knowing what I knew then, I said, "Well, I'll have to trust them, but I don't think I'll ever get the money." Because there were a lot of those verbal deals that were made that never happened. But, as it turned out, I got the money, which was wonderful, as far as I was concerned, and really honorable on the Pirates' part. So that was sort of my background in the minors. This was in 1940.

I graduated from Alhambra High School in June, and signed with the Pirates, but didn't play that year. My first year in baseball was 1941. I went to spring training with the Pirates. One of the interesting things about that era in baseball, I was in spring training as a member of the Pittsburgh Pirates and participating in the training exercises. But they wouldn't let me bat.

The only way you could take batting practice was if the players that were the regular players on the team would allow you to get in the batting cages. This shows you what baseball was in those days. There were no coaches to make your way for you. You either had to fight your way in, and as it turned out, the star of the Pirate team was a fellow named Bob Elliot, who, later on, was the MVP with the Boston Braves. I think it was 1947, he was the MVP. And he'd been traded away, so he said, "Kid, you get in there and hit, ahead of me." So that's how I got my batting practice. The game has changed considerably since that time.

I was in the minors at Albany my two first years. My second year at Albany, I led the Eastern League in home run hitting. I had 14 home runs. That doesn't sound like much, but in that league, it was a dead ball with some real great pitchers and to name two, Warren Spahn and Allie Reynolds were in that league. And the lights were very bad and the ball was dead and the parks were big. In 1942, only one fellow in the league hit .300.

December 7, 1941, the Japanese bombed Pearl Harbor. I was scheduled to play in the ball game in the afternoon, baseball game, semipro baseball game in the afternoon. So the war hit and I played that afternoon. And the next week—I really believe it was a Monday—I went down and signed up to join the program, the V-12, V-5 program of the Navy, which was to get me into being a Navy flier.

All my friends did the same thing. They signed up or were drafted. That was a big experience, and, of course, the two and a half years in the service, I probably played, I would guess, somewhere around ten baseball games. I was always at the wrong place at the wrong time for baseball, trying to learn to be a pilot. Ironically, a Hall of Fame baseball player, one of the greatest players of all time, was a teacher for me, how to play soccer.

His name was Charlie Gehringer. And we had played, well, it's part of our exercises was playing soccer. He was my coach. He was one of the greatest, if not the greatest, second basemen around. So that was sort of the background of my service thing. I got my wings, I ended up flying, but never saw much action. And we were doing air-sea rescue. I flew seaplanes. Two-engine seaplanes. I flew PBYs and also the Martin Mariner PBM. And I also did submarine work in patrol areas in the South Pacific.

And then I got out in December 1945. My thought immediately then was to get back in shape and get back and play baseball. In 1946, I went to spring training with the Pirates. I was really des-

Charlie Gehringer

tined to be sent to the Hollywood Stars team that they worked with in the Pacific Coast thing.

I had a tremendous spring training. I hit, I believe the number was 13 home runs in spring training. I earned the job and I opened up in center field for the Pirates in 1946. As it turned out, I led the league in home runs with 23, beating out Johnny Mize by one. I got very lucky there, because Mize got his arm broken while playing an exhibition game against the Yankees. And so he missed quite a few games and I was able to be the home run champion for that year, my first year in the major leagues. That was a club record for the Pittsburgh Pirates. Johnny Rizzo held the record, I believe, at 23. That was the most home runs ever hit by a rookie. That was how I got started in the home run title race of winning seven consecutive home run titles.

My first game was in St. Louis. We opened on the road, and I got a base hit that game. It was off Johnny Beazley, who had been an outstanding pitcher for the St. Louis Cardinals before the war and had injured his arm and was trying to make a comeback into Major League Baseball, which he really wasn't able to do. My first home run was in my third game and it was off of Howie Pollet, who was an outstanding left-handed pitcher for the St. Louis Cardinals.

I hit 369 home runs, and in my career, I never kept track of this, and I don't know if anybody ever did. I hit the home run (off Pollet) to right field and it might've been the only home run I ever hit in my life to right field.

Hank Greenberg joined the ball club in 1947. Didn't want to play. He had been sold to the Pirates because the Tigers didn't want to pay him the money he was trying to make and it was somewhere, I guess, he would get $70,000, $60,000 a year. And so they sold him and got rid of him. And he quit. He was tired of baseball. Pittsburgh talked him into coming into the Pirates.

Part of the deal was—he had to be the highest-paid player at that time, ever—part of the deal was he got X amount of money, and I believe the numbers might have been $70,000 or $80,000. He also was promised some other perks. And he also was promised a horse by John Galbreath who had the Darby Dan Stables. And he

Hank Greenberg

was promised a yearling. His wife, Carol Gimbel—it was the Gimbel family here in New York—they got married in either the end of '46 or the spring of '47.

That horse was really an inducement for him to play and sign. Incidentally, he never got the horse. But he was a very great influence on me, because the first day of spring training, he came to me. The training is over for the first day and all the players went in except Greenberg. And I was going in to shower and change uniforms. And he yelled at me. And I had never talked to Hank.

He said, "Hey, kid, how would you like to take some extra batting practice?"

I said, "Great."

And I came out and so he said, "I'm Hank Greenberg," and shook my hand.

And I said, "Well, I'm Ralph Kiner."

And he said, "Kid, I don't think you're going to ever be a great home run hitter." And I thought he was kidding me, 'cause I had led the league in home runs the year before in the National League. He had led the league in the American League with 44 home runs, and the Tigers got rid of him, because he was making too much money. I mean, this is the way the game was played in those days.

So anyway, he said, "I think you stand too far from the plate in the batter's box. And to be a home run hitter, you have to pull the ball," and et cetera. And so he started to work with me. He gave me some tremendous work ethic habits of doing extra work at batting and all these things. He taught me what was really the greatest things I ever found out about baseball. As Yogi would've said, he "learned me his experience." Yogi said that's what he did when he was talking about Bill Dickey, who was teaching him how to catch.

Well, I changed my whole batting approach because of Greenberg. I got on top of the plate and I had trouble. And it was a total adjustment. I worked and I worked. And I stayed with it. The one thing which is really interesting, I believe, is you've got to believe that the guy who's talking to you knows what he's talking about. There's so much false information out there, and so many people that think they know what they're doing but they don't—that you can be totally confused and be on the wrong track.

Greenberg had all the credentials. I mean, he had hit 58 home runs. He had driven in 183 runs in one season. He had all the credentials. He was one of the greatest hitters of all time. I believed him. He said, "This is going to work." And it took a lot of belief, because I was at the lowest point of my whole baseball career when it finally clicked in. And then, all of a sudden, I couldn't do anything wrong.

And it had to be because his theories were right. But it takes time, and I think one of the most important things I learned about that, you're not going to change overnight. It doesn't happen that fast. If there's going to be a change, it's going to take a lot of hard work, which I believed it did from that day on, when he joined the club. And even then, it might not work. But you've got to at least believe that it's going to work and be on the right track.

Also, Hank and I became extremely close friends. He was the best man in my wedding and we were close from that time on. He was such a great intellect and he knew more about baseball than anybody I ever talked to or ever saw. He just more or less took me under his wing and treated me like a younger brother—

Of course, as a ballplayer, when he broke in, Jewish ballplayers were treated like Jackie Robinson was treated. An interesting story about Hank was when Robinson first played his first game in Pittsburgh, the first time we saw Jackie. I had known Jackie from California. Hank ran out to him. Robinson was just getting vilified and just murdered by the other players and whatever.

Hank went out there and said to him at first base—Robinson was playing first base—he said, "Jackie," he says, "hang in there. You're going to make it." He says, "I had to go through the same thing, as a Jewish ballplayer in the major leagues." And, of course, Jackie made it big and Hank was influential, I'm sure, in Jackie's battle against the prejudice that was around at that time in Major League Baseball. Not all the players, but the Southern players really got to it. And that was their culture, their upbringing at that time.

I was raised in Southern California, and we didn't have that problem that they had in the South. The blacks were treated basically almost like the whites were. And Robinson was one of the greatest athletes of all time. In my mind, I thought he was the greatest athlete that ever played baseball. He was one of the greatest football players that ever played football in college. He was one of the greatest track men that ever played. He held the college record in what we call broad jumping now, they called it the long jump.

He was an outstanding basketball player. And so he had all those sports covered. And he was also one of the greatest competitors I ever saw.

Well, the thing about Jackie Robinson breaking in, what really impressed me was in the spring of 1947, for the first time, the Pirates trained in Florida. We had been training in California. And in

1947, we trained in Miami, Florida. He joined the Brooklyn Dodgers. And all of a sudden, he's playing baseball in the major leagues and the crowds are unreal.

I mean, and black people are walking to the ballpark and watching his games. And they drew nobody, you know, to speak of, for spring training games. Eight thousand, 9,000 would be a big crowd. In the parks that could hold the people, they were drawing 20,000, 25,000 people. And two places I remember well when we played Jackie Robinson was New Orleans. And they had a crowd. You couldn't believe that city and what took place with him in Major League Baseball. And also, Atlanta, Georgia. They had standing room only crowds in these cities. Now, when the season opened in Brooklyn, they opened with Jackie Robinson at first base. They didn't have a sell-out crowd at all. I think they had 13,000 people in the ballpark. When he first came to Pittsburgh, he didn't draw anything unusual in crowds. He drove maybe—I'm guessing now, because it's a long time ago—but they maybe had 10,000 or 13,000 in a ballpark. It really wasn't the change in the major league cities, as it was in the South. That's the one thing I really remember about him.

And of course, the other things, that's the way they were, we had to stay at different hotels at that time, which, thank God, it changed.

Well, I think, in a way, he changed baseball, inasmuch as it was an individual change with his personality and his way of playing. His ability to run and stop and go, and what-have-you, and stealing bases, was there. But in 1947, the game of baseball, especially in Brooklyn, with Duke Snider and Gil Hodges and the power hitters they had, was not to steal that many bases. And Pee Wee Reese had led the ball club in stolen bases, I think.

When he (Jackie) led the National League, it was with 20-some stolen bases, a small amount as you would think of it today. I think individually, he didn't change the style of the game being played in the major leagues that much. But his individual style was really different than anybody that we had ever seen. I hadn't seen Cobb, but

I've assumed he played somewhat like Jackie played. He had 96 stolen bases in that year, back in the early 1900s.

There was no question in my mind that Jackie, if they had been stealing bases at that time, would have held the record. He was unbelievable in his talent as a runner, and he was so agile that it was unbelievable.

I believe the reason why Branch Rickey was the man that got into the, as they called them then, the colored leagues, because they came cheap and they were available and they had great talent.

Amazingly, and this has never really been brought out by anybody that played in that era. I played a lot of baseball in the wintertime against Satchel Paige and black players that played in Southern California. As a matter of fact, I hit a home run off Paige when I was in high school, at seventeen. But I had the chances to play against them.

The thinking at that time, the consensus, was that black players were show people and wonderful to watch, but not the type of players that would be major league players who had to play every day, for winning, which was totally wrong, as it turned out. But that's what people thought about the colored leagues. And of course, they had great stars, and they had records that were fantastic, but the story was the records were not really records, because they didn't keep them accurately, or whatever. These are stories, not the truth.

And so, when Jackie hit the scene, all of a sudden, people started to change their mind about the talent that they had, and the ability. And the National League took advantage of that.

When I went to Pittsburgh for the first time, we had opened our season in St. Louis. And they played the day game on Sunday and took the train. And we also always traveled by train or bus. No airplanes at that time. And we took the train from St. Louis to Pittsburgh, which was a pretty long ride. And we arrived in Pittsburgh the next day, at about 10:00 in the morning. The train had Pullman berths and that was a great experience for me.

I had taken trains before from L.A. to the South and also to the East, but we arrived around 10:00 in the morning in Pittsburgh, and it was like midnight. I got off the train and I couldn't believe it. There was so much soot in the air, from the burning of soft coal and it was like midnight. And it was also very dirty. And there was the smog in the air, and soot, and what-have-you.

I couldn't believe it. I had come from California where they didn't have smog at that time. Mostly orange trees and orange groves, and things like that, and beautiful weather and everything. I went to the hotel and I said I didn't like this. Now, I went to the ballpark for the first time, never having seen Forbes Field. And I walked in the ballpark and I looked down the left line. It was 365 feet away. The center field fence was 456 feet away. I looked at that and that smog and the weather conditions and I thought, "This is the worst thing I have ever done in my life," I said, "I'm on the wrong team."

That was another reason why I owe a debt of gratitude to Hank Greenberg, because they shortened the fence in left field and they called it "Greenberg Gardens." And they took it from 365 down the left field line to 335, which was a normal distance. And then, when Hank retired, they had to rename it and somebody thought of the name with two K's, Kiner's Korner.

And they renamed it Kiner's Korner. And when Branch Rickey came over as a GM and traded me to the Cubs, he tried to take down that fence in the middle of the season and they wouldn't let him. He had to wait until the end of the season, because there was a rule in baseball, you couldn't alter the field during the season's play.

Because Bill Veeck, at one time, wanted to change the fences when the Yankees came to town, and move them way back. And they wouldn't let him do that.

In 1947, I hit 51 home runs. That was the result of Greenberg working with me. This is a very interesting story. Our manager of the Pirates in 1947, I should say, was Billy Herman. In the beginning of the season, I was hitting terribly. And Herman wanted to send me back to the minor leagues. And Greenberg went in to

Johnny Mize

Franklin Kenny, who was the president of the Pirates at that time, before John Galbreath. And Hank Greenberg went to Kenny and said, "Don't send this kid out." He went to the front office and said, "Don't send this kid out. He's going to be all right." Well, going into the end of the last day, I had three home runs, which is nothing.

And there are reasons that make sense that Billy Herman didn't think I was going to be a ballplayer and send me out. So I can't blame him. And Hank had made this intervention on my part. And on the last day of May, I struck out four times in one game against Hank Borowy, who was with the Cubs at that time. And that was the lowest point of my life. I knew I was going to go out and my dream was going to go up in smoke.

And the next day, June 1, I had two home runs in the game, and from June 1 to the end of the season, I had 47 home runs. Johnny Mize and I tied that year, with 51 home runs. We were tied for second most home runs in the history of the National League. Hack Wilson had hit 56 in 1930.

I don't remember the pitchers, but I know I had some unbelievable streaks. I had seven home runs in three games, twice. I'm still the only man to hit eight home runs in four games. And they were unbelievable. I do remember a story about Red Barrett, pitcher for the Boston Braves coming in. I had a chance to set a new record for home runs in consecutive games. And he made a statement that Kiner wasn't going to hit any home runs off him. Well, I had to hit two to have the eight. I hit two home runs off him in that game. So he didn't pop off anymore after that. But I did get that streak going.

I beat out Mize in my first year with 23. He had 22. And the next year, we tied at 51. The next year, we tied at 40. And then, I outlasted him. He was getting older and he moved over to the Yankees, so he wasn't a real competitor in the home run race with me. And then, of course, the next year, I had 54. That would've been pretty tough to beat.

We drew a lot of people. That was the main thing. In 1947, the Pirates broke a million for the first time. That was the year I had 51 home runs. We were drawing a million four right through that period of time, which, for a club that finished either last or next to last, other than 1948, when we finished fourth, we were really packing the people in the stands.

I was, for the time of being there and the time of baseball, I was paid well by the Pirates. At one time, I was the highest-paid player in the National League, with $90,000. And then, Musial came along and said, "I'm a better player than Kiner and I want ninety-one."

And Busch said to him, "We'll give you one hundred." And he was the first $100,000 ballplayer in the National League.

DiMaggio and Williams were making about the same, somewhere around $100,000 at that time.

If you put it in perspective and go back to the days of, say, Ty

Cobb, where no one drew a million people, a big season might've been 400,000 people at the ballpark. Cobb, a great baseball player, could do things that, in his time, were better than anyone else.

But the progression of baseball with Babe Ruth had finally changed in the swing of the game of baseball, from a game where you hit the ball in a line and tried to beat out hits and hit for a high average and steal bases. And the crowd got to be following Babe Ruth. And the home runs started to make bigger and better crowds. And then, it wasn't unusual for attendance now to be two million people. And then, it got to three and then into four million, in one season.

So it's all part of the game and progression. At one time in baseball, the catcher didn't wear a glove, didn't wear a mask, and didn't wear shin guards. So I guess you've just got to say it's all part of the way things are and I sure wouldn't want to be driving a Model T Ford, when they've got Cadillacs and everything out there.

One pitcher I particularly remember is Satchel Paige, especially in California, because he pitched out there every winter, and he was awesome. His reputation preceded him, because he was regarded as the greatest pitcher that ever lived black or white, by a lot of people. And so, when I played him, it was at Wrigley Field, where the L.A. Angels played their games in the Pacific Coast League.

Later on, when they expanded, the California Angels played in that ballpark. It was a pretty good-sized major league ballpark. They would seat about 25,000 people there. So I hit against him and I'm a kid and I'm seventeen. And I don't know who, you know, I'm scared to death. This guy's going to be—you won't see the ball. I mean, in my mind, it was there. Earlier in the interview, I said I hit my first homer in the major leagues in right field.

I hit my first home run really against Satchel Paige to right field. And now, the interesting story is that Buck O'Neil was on that ball club with Satchel Paige that day. And then, later on, he's with the Cubs as a coach. He told me this story. When I hit that home run off Satchel Paige to right field, Paige, when he came in, said, "Who hit that home run off me?"

And Buck O'Neil said, "Well, that was a kid that's playing baseball in high school. He hit a home run off you."

He says, "What's his number?"

He says, "He's wearing number 4."

He said, "Tell me when number 4 comes up again."

So I came up again and he struck me out. I mean, you know, I wasn't going to do it twice. And I wouldn't have done it twice, either. Later on, I saw him when he pitched in the major leagues at a very old age.

But one thing about him that I remember, he had immaculate control. And he could throw a ball anywhere he wanted to and he also was extremely fast. I don't think he was as fast as Bob Feller, but he was fast enough. He had great control. He threw kind of sidearm, kind of almost like Walter Johnson, kind of a slingshot-type throwing. And he had a very hard curveball, very short and very fast.

The way he warmed up for ball games, he would take infield at third base and then go out and pitch. No one I ever knew ever did that.

People have asked me who was the toughest pitcher I ever hit against. I mean, there's no argument whatsoever. Ewell Blackwell. Most of the people say, "Ewell who?" And I said, "Ewell Blackwell." And they said, "Never heard of him." Well, in 1947, he won 16 games in a row. He won over 20 games. He almost pitched back-to-back no-hitters. He pitched a no-hitter against the Boston Braves. He came down to Brooklyn. And Eddie Stanky got a base hit through his legs in the ninth inning, with one man out, or he would've duplicated Vander Meer's feat of back-to-back no-hitters.

Ewell Blackwell threw about 98 miles an hour, sidearm, out of here, and was mean on top of it. And he wouldn't hesitate to knock you down. The thing about him was, you couldn't find the ball, because it would come out of third base, and before you could find the ball to pick it up, it was almost on top of you, which made it seem like he's throwing 200 miles an hour.

He was, to my mind, the toughest that I ever hit against. I think that the greatest pitcher I ever saw was Bob Feller. Feller had a 100-mile-an-hour fastball and a curveball that never stopped.

The closest to him, I guess, was Nolan Ryan, of the modern-day players. But all the pitchers, you know, all the good pitchers—Warren Spahn was a great pitcher. And if a modern-day person, if they saw Sandy Koufax, Warren Spahn pitched the same way Sandy Koufax did. Warren Spahn, of course, won more games than any left-hand pitcher in the history of baseball. And he won 20 games for 13 straight—maybe not straight years, but 13 years. And didn't win a game until he was twenty-six. But you see him now, you say, "That man couldn't pitch at all." He doesn't look like he ever could pitch.

But he was tough. But pitchers like Allie Reynolds and Bob Lemon and the great pitchers, they were all tough. They were all really challenges. In some sense, the easiest pitcher to hit against, and not the worst pitcher, but the easiest to hit against, was Robin Roberts. It looked easy. But he was also the hardest to hit. He had a fastball that would just rise and when he could add on, when he was in a jam and throw the ball faster when he had to get you out.

And in those times, he was almost impossible to hit. But he was very easy to hit against. But you wouldn't get any hits. It was comfortable to hit against him.

It was extremely difficult to play with losing teams. In a way, I got some vicarious thrills out of the Mets in their good years, as a broadcaster. There was nothing better than to go out and have a good day and win a ball game. And I can't say there's nothing worse than having a good day and losing a ball game, because you offset it somewhat, because you had to have had a chance to help try and win. But losing, day after day, is the worst thing in the world.

Of course, you miss a lot of acclaim that way, because, like, one game, I hit two home runs in Ebbets Field. I think I hit it off of Carl Erskine, and I drove in, like, seven or eight runs. In the end, we got beat 12–11, or maybe it was 13–12, or whatever. And you lost that ball game. Well, if we had won the game, then you feel great.

But even though you have a chance to and you've done well, it's not the same. I never got a chance to play in the World Series. I did, of course, play in some All-Star Games, which is always a great thrill and a great challenge. In the All-Star Games, there's electricity in there, and I got that electricity with the Mets, as a broadcaster. And I broadcast World Series games, which is not quite the same, but it's still there. But playing on losing teams is not very good. It's no fun.

When Branch Rickey came over to be the GM of the Pittsburgh Pirates, I knew I was going to go. His philosophy was don't pay a lot of money out and make sure that you trade off—his theory, which isn't a bad theory, really, when you think about it—it's better to trade a player a year too soon than a year too late. And so I knew I was going to go. And he came over the end of the 1952 season.

And in '52, we had the worst team you could have. We lost 112

Branch Rickey

games that year. And we had high school players playing on our team. We had Bobby del Greco, who had just graduated from high school, a center fielder. And the first baseman had graduated from high school and was playing first base. And it was really a bad team. And we finished last and lost 112 games.

So I knew that sooner or later, I was going to be out of there. So in '53, there was a lot of talk about trades and it more or less boiled down to I was going to go to maybe Brooklyn, maybe Cincinnati, maybe the Cubs. It was all hassled around in spring training also, in the early part of the season. I was really rooting for Chicago, because I really didn't hit that well in Cincinnati.

It was a real tough park to hit in, for some reason. Brooklyn, I would've liked, but I didn't think that was going to be reality. And that would've been fine. Chicago played all day ball at that time and I thought I'd enjoy day baseball better than the night ball. So I knew it was going to be sooner or later, I was going to get it. And in the winter of '52, I got my contract from Rickey and he cut my salary 25 percent, which is the largest salary cut he could do.

And of course, I argued back and forth, through the mail and also wire, Western Union, and things like that. I really didn't get much done. It was still 25 percent cut. We argued back and forth. And finally, Branch Rickey said, "Son, where'd we finish?"

And I said, "We finished last."

He said, "We can finish last without you." Which meant I either took what he offered or I wouldn't play baseball.

I was single all this time. Well, I didn't get married until I was twenty-seven, and so when the Pirates were bought by Bing Crosby, I got then to meet with him and see him and I, of course, had played golf with him in Palm Springs before that. But I knew him better and one day, a coach of the Pirates, a guy named John McKee, and I went out to watch Crosby make a movie.

And interestingly, you know, making a movie takes a lot of time and they have to use doubles and stand-ins and all this sort of thing. And Crosby in the studio, which is a big studio, had a big carpet on the wall, and he would hit golf balls into this carpet while they were getting the scenes set. So anyway, we talked with him. He was always a tremendous sports fan and a great golfer. He was a scratch player and won club championships and everything else. And he said, "How would you like to have a date with Elizabeth Taylor?"

I thought he was kidding me and I said, "Well, why not?"

And he said, "Well, I'll set it up for you." So he got his PR man, whatever it was. I think they were both with Paramount at that time. And he arranged for me to contact her. And I contacted her. And we were going to a movie called *Twelve O'Clock High*. They premiered the movie in Hollywood. And it was an old-fashioned premiere. They had people sitting on the street on Hollywood Boulevard in bleachers. And they had klieg lights going all around the sky. And I went over to pick her up at her house. She was living with her mother and father.

And I was driving a Cadillac with the top down. I thought I was going to really impress her. And she was late. And I sat there talking with her father for about half an hour. And finally, she was ready to go. And we get in and I drive to the Grauman's Chinese Theatre, where they had this premiere. And as it turned out, we were the last ones to get in the theater. And the man that took my car said, "What's your name?"

And I said, "Ralph Kiner."

He says, "Okay. I'm taking your car."

And when we went in and it was really a festive thing. Interviewed by the top Hollywood writers, and things like that. Well, we saw the movie, came out. And I'm sitting there and I hear this guy on the PA system say, "Mr. Gary Cooper's car, please." And I guess the car would drive up and then they'd say somebody else.

So I finally went up to them. I said, "Would you page my car?"

And he said, "What's your name?"

And I said, "Ralph Kiner." So okay.

And he says, "Mr. Ralph Kiner's car, please." And we stood there and waited and waited and waited. And now, it's getting late. Crowds are thinning out. And now, I'm getting a little bit hot.

And I finally got up and went to him and said, "Would you page my car again?"

He says, "Well, your chauffeur must've fallen asleep."

I looked at him and I said, "Chauffeur? I don't have a chauffeur."

He said, "Well, then your car is out there." And he pointed to a vacant lot about one hundred yards away. And so here I go, walking with Elizabeth Taylor on my arm in a tuxedo. And she's got a gown on. And we walk to the car. Needless to say, that was my last date with her. We went to a place called Romanoff's. It was "the" place to go in Hollywood, and a supper club, that type of thing.

And Louella Parsons came by. Well, she could make or break anybody in Hollywood. She was a great columnist that wrote about the stars and whatever. And so, she came up to Elizabeth Taylor and said, "Who's your date tonight?"

And she said, "This is Ralph Kiner."

And she said, "Oh? What does he do?"

And she said, "Well, he plays for the Pittsburgh Pirates." Well, it so happened that that next day, on Sunday—this was a Saturday night—the Pittsburgh Steeler football team was playing the Rams in the Coliseum.

And so she thought I was with that team and she said, "Well, I hope your team wins tomorrow." So that was kind of a disaster.

I got started with the Mets as a broadcaster in '62. I kind of joked about it, and then someone said, "Well, how did you get picked for the Mets job?"

I said, "Because they saw who I played with all my life and I had a losing record." Incidentally, the Mets, in that year of 1962, broke the record set by the Pirates, of 112 losses. They lost 120.

But we didn't expect a whole lot and none of the people did. And two things, I think, made a difference. One, the people in New York were so happy to get National League baseball back in the town. They would've taken anything, which they really got. And the other was Casey Stengel. Casey Stengel made it so easy to lose those games, in a way, that he always had something to say, would take the onus off of the losses. And nobody expected much, and they got nothing. But Stengel was the guy they got that made the difference.

Well, my first story about Casey—and there are so many that you couldn't tell them all—was of my first broadcast with him. It wasn't called the *Kiner's Korner,* which I have done over the years, but it was just a postgame show. And we'd played our first game at the Polo Grounds and I had to have Casey as my guest on the show. Now, I had never done baseball TV. And I had done radio with the White Sox, but not TV, and so I was apprehensive about how Casey would be.

And as you know, being around Casey, he never stopped talking, so you'd never know where the end was. And in television, you had to get off the air on a specific minute.

And I'm doing the thing and everything's going pretty well. He was fabulous this way. He knew your job and he would work with you. And he knew what you were trying to get, and he would do this. Now, the next thing I'm worried about is to get him off the air. And so, he stopped at the right time. He knew that, too. And so I thank him. I say, "Casey, it's really wonderful for you to be on my first show, and I wish you luck," and whatever I said.

And he says, "Thank you very much," and gets up and walks off. Well, unfortunately for me and the crew that worked the show, he's still got the lavalier on around his neck, for the audio, and he tears the whole set down. It all collapses. And now, my assistant director is standing there. He's petrified, because he's got to get it back up, or he has to get off the air.

And finally, I said something. I really don't remember what I said, "We'll be back in just a minute after this commercial," or whatever. So anyway, it's a minute or two minutes and we're back. And I said good-bye and that was my first show with Casey Stengel.

The greatest thing that ever happened to me, as far as being a baseball player and being around and knowing all the great baseball players from the era of, say, 1930 on, I did get to meet Babe Ruth. I did get to meet Ty Cobb. I met Babe Ruth from the film *Pride of the Yankees*. He played the part of Babe Ruth in that movie. Babe Herman was the fellow that got me there, a great player for the Brooklyn Dodgers.

He was trying to sign me as a high school player. He took me down and introduced me to Babe Ruth. Of course, Ruth didn't know who I was. That was the only time I met him. I met Ty Cobb at ball games at the Hollywood field, Gilmore Stadium. I met him several times and got to know him a little bit. Even in that era of baseball, I got to know people. I met Connie Mack. And so I met all of these people from all along, way back in baseball.

It's been a celebrating experience for me. I mean, it's just been a great life.

The one question that they asked me, "Who was the greatest player you ever saw?" I didn't see Cobb play, or Babe Ruth, or any of those guys. But it's impossible to answer. I might've changed my mind one or two times as to who I thought was the greatest player. I think I would say, not having seen Ruth, the best hitter I ever saw was Ted Williams.

I could be wrong. I mean, no one talks about Stan Musial. There's no question about Stan Musial being as close to him, or ahead of him, or what. Stan Musial was a fantastic hitter. Maybe the best all-around player, boy, I get into all kinds of arguments on this, especially with my broadcast partner, Fran Healy. He says Mays. I say DiMaggio.

And now I'm in trouble because it's almost impossible not to pick Mays. And my answer is that the one thing that DiMaggio did better than anybody that ever lived that could hit a ball hard, home-run-type hitter, was not to strike out. He put the ball in play. In 1941, he struck out 13 times in the entire season. He was putting that ball in play all the time. And when that ball's in play, there's something that's going to happen. And that's why I would take DiMaggio. Talent-wise, I think Mays is the best I ever saw. But if I had to pick—and to me, first of all, you'd be lucky to have a pick of DiMaggio or Mays. I mean, either one, you can't go wrong. I think I'd pick DiMaggio. I don't know. Tough to say.

And then, of course, you've got Hank Aaron. I mean, we'd leave him out, why? I don't know. This is a guy, you know, hit all those home runs and was a great hitter for years and years and years. I mean, he's a fantastic player. And he was also a great fielder. And I'm sure you wouldn't leave out Frank Robinson. My goodness. What a player he was. I mean, his numbers are amazing. And you don't hear much about him. And the one player—I didn't really see him play; I saw him play at the very end of his career—that nobody talks about, Jimmie Foxx. Well, I mean, his numbers are unreal. He hit 56 home runs in one year.

And his RBIs were fantastic. And the guy could do everything. He could catch. He could play third. He could play the outfield. He even pitched.

Baseball today? The gloves are so good now that you practically cannot drop a ball. That makes hitting tougher. The other factors are factors in the game. The ball is lighter. I don't care what they say. There's no question about it. The bats are even better, which I didn't believe for a long time, and now I do. The parks are definitely smaller. And the pitching is stretched out. You still have great pitching, but again, the offset of maybe the relief pitching being better than it was when we played can offset some of that. There's intangibles that are hard to add up.

I was extremely fortunate to be able to do the one thing I wanted to do as a kid, which was to be in baseball, and to be able to do it over, probably, a longer period of time than anybody that ever was in the game of baseball.

MONTE IRVIN

Monte Irvin had a fine career, but it may be that major league fans didn't get to see him at his best. Because of the "color line," the renowned left fielder didn't make his big league debut until after his thirtieth birthday. "Most of the black ballplayers thought Monte Irvin should have been the first black in the major leagues," said Cool Papa Bell, a Negro League star. "Monte was our best young ball player at the time. He could hit the long ball; he had a great arm; he could field; he could run. Yes, he could do everything." After a distinguished career in the Negro Leagues, the thirty-one-year-old Irvin made his major league debut in 1949 with the New York Giants.

By 1951, Irvin's offensive numbers were among the best in the game—174 hits, .312 batting average, 24 home runs, and a league-best 121 RBI—helping him finish third in the senior circuit's MVP voting. That was also the year the Giants made a late-season charge against the Brooklyn Dodgers, one of the most famous pennant races in the game's history. Irvin was a key figure down the stretch. Then, after the Giants' playoff victory over the Dodgers, he batted .458 in a losing effort against the Yankees in the World Series.

Hall of Fame pitcher Carl Hubbell saw firsthand Irvin's importance: "I don't think there ever was a better hitter than Irvin was those last two months. It seemed that every time he came to bat with men on base, he delivered." Stan Musial, who finished second in the MVP voting behind Roy Campanella that year, said, "Monte Irvin has had a terrific year with the Giants. I wouldn't be surprised if he was named Most Valuable Player

in the National League. As far as I'm concerned, he's earned it." Cam-
panella said, "As great as he was in 1951, he was twice that good ten years
earlier in the Negro Leagues. He was much faster and a far better hitter."

According to Yankees pitcher Allie Reynolds, "We pitched to Irvin
every way we could think of, but he hit whatever we threw with equal
ability. We went over to him at length in our clubhouse meetings, and
worked on him inside and outside, high and low. But no system seemed to
bother him. He is one of the greatest natural hitters I have seen in a long
time."

Irvin's career was honored when he was elected to the Hall of Fame in
1973. "Irvin's not in the Hall of Fame because of what he did in the ma-
jors. He's in there because of what he did in the Negro Leagues. I played
with him there and he deserved to come to the majors long before he fi-
nally did," said pitcher Don Newcombe.

I WAS BORN IN ALABAMA, raised in New Jersey—East Orange,
New Jersey. And I—when I came to Newark in 1927, I think I was
eight years old. And I was in grade school; we had a baseball team.
Since I was a little bigger than the rest of the kids, and strong, and
everything else, I was a pitcher. And later on, I played the shortstop;
I caught; I played third base; I played first base. So I got a chance
to—to really get a full run of most of the positions. And I just had a
feeling I had a flair for baseball. Not only could I throw very hard, I
could run, and I could hit, and I just loved it. And later on, when I
got in high school, getting older, you know, stronger, it just like
came natural for me. And again, I just loved it.

I went to a couple of years in college, Lincoln University in Ox-
ford, Pennsylvania. I played four sports, but baseball was the one I
really liked the best. And, now, at that time, in order for me not to
lose my amateur standing, I played under an assumed name; and
I'm joining the Newark Eagles, which is the local team. We played
there at the Ruppert Stadium in Newark, and when we would go on
the road, I would play. But at home, I come to the stadium, work

Monte Irvin

out, and then go sit in the stands. So like that, until I left school—
left school in 1939. Nobody ever knew that I was playing a little
professional game ball. It gave me a chance to, I don't know, maybe
earn $100 a month.

I played under the name of Jimmy Nelson. Jimmy Nelson was a
friend of mine. Jimmy might still be alive. I've been looking for
him. He was about the same age. He was a catcher, a great physique,
great arm, and he was just what I wanted to be like. So that was the
reason why I—I took his name. And, now, I'm playing with the Eagles—Newark Eagles—that's the local team, in the Negro League.
And getting better. So I played with the Eagles until, well, 1942.
Then I got an offer in 1942 to play ball in Mexico. A fellow by the
name of Jorge Pasquel, who was the—who was the father of Mexi-

can baseball, offered me $500 a month, and $250 for an apartment and a maid. So what I did, my wife and I—we got married—and we went to Mexico, and I played there all of the 1942 season. One of the most wonderful times I've ever had in baseball. In fact, I hit .397 that season. And so I played there until last of October. I came on back to Newark after it was all over. And in 1943 I was inducted into the Army.

The team there in Newark, they had the some wonderful stars. They had Willie Wells, who is a Hall of Famer; we had Ray Dandridge, who is a Hall of Famer; we had Leon Day, a Hall of Famer; Raleigh "Biz" Mackey; all of these fellows were stars. So we knew we couldn't ever think about correct playing major league because we knew there's no chance. So we wanted to be the best we could be,

Willie Wells

though, in the Negro League. It gave us a chance to travel around. Every year they had an East-West game in Chicago that was like the All-Star Game, which was just a wonderful event. So I never thought before World War II that we could ever play in the major league.

My heroes in the Negro League were: Josh Gibson, Buck Leonard, Satchel Paige, Cool Papa Bell, Oscar Charleston. These are all great players. And we would go to see them play, and so we wanted to play and be like them. When Jackie broke the color barrier, that was the end of the Negro Leagues because the fans, now, were not too interested in the local team. They wanted to see Jackie play and the others who followed: Roy Campanella, Don New combe, Minnie Minoso. I'm so happy that Jackie did a great job in pioneering because it made it better for those who came after. In fact, it made it better, not only in baseball, but in all sports like football, basketball, and golf, tennis, and so on.

In the Negro Leagues we traveled in a bus from one city to another. For instance, on a Sunday, we might play in Newark, New Jersey; that Monday we might be playing in Washington, D.C. From Washington, D.C., we might go on down to Richmond, and then we worked our way right on down south. We played in Birmingham, Alabama, and then New Orleans, Houston, Dallas, San Antonio, like that, playing other Negro League teams. We were just happy to get away from home, and, of course, in the winter league, you want to play well, so that you get invited back. And so the saying became, "Playing baseball is better than working." Of course, we would have played for nothing almost, and we did play almost for nothing, but it was very, very enjoyable. And then, as I mentioned before, when Jackie broke the color barrier, now, we knew that there might be a chance to make some real money.

After the World Series you were permitted to barnstorm for a month and Bob Feller was free-thinking enough to play the Satchel Paige All-Stars. They had two planes, and they would fly from one city to another. They made a lot of money. In fact, they made more money for barnstorming for that month than they did in the regular season. So when we played these fellows, we wanted to prove that we did belong. And so we would shine our shoes a little longer, you know, make sure our caps weren't streaked, make sure the uniform fit, and that we would go out and really try to prove that, if given a chance, we could also be major leaguers. And I guess, out of about 30 games, I guess, it was almost half-and-half, 15-15. But it did prove that if given the right training and given the opportunity, that we could make it. So Bob—I can pay tribute to him. Bob Feller was partially responsible for Branch Rickey and all the others because we got exposed, played before big crowds and it was now a new market for talent. You know, maybe the major league is now looking for guys who could play. And here is all the talent in the Negro Leagues.

Before the world war, World War II, I had been selected by the heads of the Negro Leagues and the NAACP to put pressure on the government to integrate baseball because I was second to none. I could hit, run, throw, field, hit with power, had a little education, plus my high school was integrated. I played with Italian kids, Irish, German, all down the line. But then this is right after the war, they said, "If these fellows can go to Europe and go to the Pacific and fight for you, why can't they play for you? Why can't they play baseball for you?" And so that was a big—one of the bigger reasons why Branch Rickey decided to do it.

Jackie had been in the Army. He had never played serious baseball. After he got out of the Army he played, I think, maybe a month or two with the Kansas City Monarchs. And that was the only experience that he had. He played shortstop and they found that he just didn't have the arm for shortstop. So they really took a chance and signed him. Why Branch Rickey decided, I just don't know. I had a discussion with some friends of mine. I said, if it had been me, if I had to make that choice, I would have selected Roy Campanella, because Roy was a star catcher, a great hitter, and home run hitter. Great arm. Great in calling pitches. Great in blocking pitches. And just an all-around nice person. Nobody disliked Roy Campanella. He had that way about him to get along with people. He kept you laughing, the way he told stories and so on. He was such a star. And he had been proven for ten years. Here Jackie was fairly brand-new. Why Branch took the chance, I still don't know. But as it turned out, he made the right choice. Because when Jackie got the chance, he improved himself. He moved over from shortstop to second base. Of course he played first base a little bit but they had Gil Hodges over there. And then they traded Eddie Stanky to the Braves so Jackie was a regular second baseman and he and Pee Wee hooked up for a great double play combination. So every year now he got a little better. He became a clutch hitter. He had some home run power. He was very thrilling on the bases.

And people hadn't seen anybody run the bases the way he had. He was a leader, very eloquent and educated. So Branch, I guess, saw this in Jackie and that is the reason why he signed him. And Jackie just did a great job of being the first.

Now they played a more of a running game because a lot of those guys could fly. Before, in order to get a man to second base or third base, we used to use the hit-and-run play, but now some of the men were so fast, they could just steal and we didn't have to sacrifice.

They missed the cream of the crop. When I say the cream of the crop, if they had taken the fellows say around 1932 or '33, they would have had some outstanding players. They would have got the chance to see Cool Papa Bell run. And they would have had the chance to see Oscar Charleston play. Oscar Charleston was the Willie Mays of that era. Feared no pitcher, just a wonderful, wonderful all-around baseball player. So they missed all that. They missed Raymond Brown, who pitched for the Homestead Grays, great curveball pitcher. They missed Smokey Joe Williams, fastball pitcher. Played against the major leaguers, shut them out here and there. Then they missed Leon Day, one of the best pitchers. Bob Gibson reminded me of Leon. Not only was Leon Day a great pitcher, but he was a great second baseman and he was a great outfielder. Sometimes in the late innings, they would put him in the outfield for defensive purposes. Or they'd put him in to play second base. He had catlike moves and again, a natural. And he could run like a deer. And just a great all-around player. So they missed all these fellows. They missed Raymond Dandridge playing. I wish the major league fans could have seen him play third base. He had that knack of coming and fielding that slow-hit ball down the third base line, just take it and flip it, sometimes not even looking and get the man, just like that, at first base. They missed all of that. But to the fans down in Latin America and throughout the United States, in the Negro Leagues, these guys were very well known and they were publicized and people came to see them play. And again, it is just too bad that they didn't start earlier.

I was under contract to the Newark Eagles, and Mrs. Effa Manley, who owned the Eagles with her husband, Abe, wanted some money before she would let Branch Rickey sign me. Rickey said no. She said, "Then I'll release him." And they released me from my contract and then Horace Stoneham in the New York Giants picked me up.

Effa Manley

I was making $6,000 a year now in the Negro Leagues. Minimum in the major league at that time was $5,000. So I took a $1,000 cut, but I knew in the long run, organized baseball was the place to play, and as it turned out I kept moving up. Next year, I was making $8,000 and then later on, $12,500, and then I had a great year in 1951. And owner-president Horace Stoneham called me in the office, and he says, "You know, you had a good season, and I want to, you know, I want to know how much money you want."

So I had to think real fast. I said, "Mr. Stoneham, you know, you and I had never had any problem with money. Whatever you think is fair." Just like that, threw the ball back in his court.

And he said, "Suppose I just double your salary."

And right away, I said, "Well, that's good," before he could change his mind. I said, "That's good enough for me." So I signed and—'52, '53, '54, and '55, I made a deal for $25,000. Now, the top salary at that time was about $40,000. Nobody's making more than $40,000 except maybe Ralph Kiner and Stan Musial, and Joe DiMaggio. Of course later on, $100,000 became absolute tops. We're talking about Joe DiMaggio, Ted Williams, and the usual couple of other guys, Feller.

Now I signed for $25,000 and then in spring training, playing an exhibition game in Denver, getting ready to come back east to start the season, I had a terrible accident in third base: I slid and broke my ankle. I told [manager] Leo Durocher, "I'll heal fast, and I'll be back." That was April 2, 1952, in Denver about three o'clock in the afternoon. By August the 1st, I was playing.

Willie Mays come to our club 1951. I think he was about twenty years old. I think he was hitting almost .500 up there in the Minneapolis, Minnesota, in the American Association. And you could tell right away that he was a natural—a diamond in the rough—so to speak. The way he would move, the way he would throw the ball, the way he would catch the ball, he had flair, he had charisma.

And sure enough, he didn't start off that much. I think he went to the plate maybe 13, 14, 15 times, before he got a base hit. But he caught everything that was hit in the outfield and threw everybody

Willie Mays

out that ran. He came in the clubhouse and he said, "Maybe I'm not ready, Leo, maybe you better send me back to Minneapolis."

So Leo said, "Not on your life." He said, "You're my center fielder, today, tomorrow, and forever." He said, "You just go out there and play the way you're playing." He said, "The home runs will come, the hits will come." Sure enough that was like on a Thursday. Friday night, now we open up against the Braves, the Boston Braves at that time. Warren Spahn was the pitcher. First time up, Spahn threw Willie a changeup and he hit it about 400 feet over that left field pavilion.

That year we won our first game, and I think we lost the next 11. And I think we were playing in Brooklyn, and you know, the club-houses are close there in Brooklyn, and we could hear the guys, the

Dodgers players saying, "Eat your heart out, Leo, you'll never win it this year." So Durocher would tell us, "This should be a great incentive for us to get our act together and start to play." And start to play we did. Now, we find ourselves in the middle of August, 13½ games behind. So we really started to play well, won 16 games in a row.

When we were behind, Leo never said "Let's catch them." He never said that. He always said, "Let's see how close we can come, fellows." Every day, he said, "Let's get after them." We just kept winning and kept winning, until finally we were tied. And during that streak, we had the wives cooking things that each one of us liked. We had ministers and priests lighting candles, people saying special prayers, and fans were rooting. It was just a wonderful, wonderful chase, to see if we could do it. And then when Bobby Thomson hit that home run, we realized we were the champions. One of the greatest feelings that I've ever had. It put an extra $5,000 in our pocket. That was a lot of money at the time, and going into the

Bobby Thomson's 1951 home run

World Series I noticed that as Bobby Thomson was circling the
bases, Jackie Robinson stood there with his glove in his hand
watching, I guess trying to make sure that Bob touched every base.

They said that we were getting the signs, and the Giants didn't
really win it. You didn't win it because you were doing something
illegal. Well, from the beginning of baseball, signs have been stolen
by the coaches, by somebody. We had gotten a few signs during the
course of the season but that game, we did not. We want to win it,
you know, on our own. And I remember we opened up in Brooklyn
[a three-game playoff to decide the National League pennant]. We
won the game there. They moved over to the Polo Grounds and
they beat us 10–0, and the next game, they were winning 4–1 in the
ninth inning. If we were getting the signs, we weren't doing a very
good job.

After beating the Dodgers, we didn't really have a chance to
enjoy it. Because the next day we had to report to the Yankee Stadium for the beginning of the World Series. We didn't fear the Yankees. We knew they were a good club. And we won that first game
and they beat us four games to two. But it was close. It was interesting. But again, it was a little anticlimactic because we had done this
great thing in winning the pennant against the Dodgers. So, okay,
they beat us, but you know it was just one of those, you can't win
them all. That was the feeling. We'll get them next year. And you
know the Yankees with that great staff of theirs, was just a little too
much for us. And they were lucky in certain instances. We were
going great, and then that Sunday, I remember when we really had
them on the ropes, it rained, and gave Reynolds an extra day's rest.
And he came back to beat us. You know, if it hadn't rained we might
have won the Series ourselves.

I have to mention the '54 year, too. This is when Cleveland had
won 111 games, the most ever in the regular season in the American
League. And we came in and beat them four in a row. How did that
happen? Number one, they trained, spring training in Tucson, Arizona. We trained in Phoenix, Arizona. We knew their strengths and
we knew their weaknesses. They had power. They didn't have much
speed. We were faster than they were. And we had better defense.

Now, the first game was that great catch—they call it The Catch—Willie Mays made it off Vic Wertz in deep right center field. That saved the game. And then Dusty Rhodes coming in and hitting a home run off Lemon, that won it. Now, if Willie hadn't made the catch and Dusty hadn't hit the home run and they had won that first game, they might have beat us four in a row. But once we got our momentum going, Durocher said, "You know, let's do the same thing we did yesterday. Let's go." And we won the second one and went on into Cleveland and won those two. It was real easy. They were down. They couldn't understand what had happened to them. It was just that we were lucky and they were very unlucky.

On The Catch, I was playing in left field; Mays, of course, goes into center; and Don Mueller goes to the right. When Vic Wertz comes to the plate, we had a pitcher by the name of Don Liddle, left-hander, and Mays played center field according to who the pitcher was and how they were going to pitch to the hitter. And he had Vic Wertz shaded over to left center because he didn't think that Vic could hit Don, who had a good fastball and a good curve. He didn't think that Vic could pull the ball the way he did to right center. So he was playing him over to left center. Now, when the ball was hit, Mays at the contact of the bat just took off. He ran and ran and when he did this, we knew that he was going to make the catch. He caught that ball over his shoulder, and just as remarkable was the fact that he had the presence of mind to wheel and throw the ball back to keep Larry Doby from scoring all the way from second base on the sacrifice fly. And that was the key point in the game.

So now on the way in, I said to him, "Hey, Roomy, I didn't think you were going to get to that one."

He said, "Are you kidding? I had it all the way."

I said, "You did, huh?"

If I had to pick an All-Star team from both worlds, position by position, who were the best that I saw? At first base you got to have Lou Gehrig. But Buck Leonard was just as good and nobody knew about Buck. Second base I would have to go for Rogers Hornsby. Second base, you know in the Negro League because Jackie Robinson started, he's a great second baseman. I like, one of my favorite players is Joe Morgan. Great, run like a deer. Great home run power and all of that. Great announcer now. Shortstop. Okay. The best shortstop they say was Honus Wagner, but I never saw him play. But you know it was generally agreed that he was just a great shortstop. I played with a fellow by the name of Willie Wells that played just like Ozzie Smith. Ozzie has no peers as a fielder. Willie Wells played the same way, but just a little better hitter than Ozzie. Now on third base I played with Dandridge. But Dandridge did not have the home run power of Mike Schmidt, or Brooks Robinson. So you would have to go there. Now, the greatest catcher, well in the majors, you have Mickey Cochrane. I played with Josh and I always said you can't get any better than he was. So now in the outfield, well my favorite player before the war was Joe DiMaggio. I used to just love to see Joe play center field and you know the way he caught the ball and the flair that he had and was very smooth and so on. But who can play center field any better than Willie Mays?

Now, you have Babe Ruth at right. Hank Aaron just broke Babe's record and Hank was a great fielder, great, stole a lot of bases. You know, great arm. All right. Now, in left field, you have Ted Williams. Wonderful hitter. And Frank Robinson, a terrific ballplayer. Could steal, could hit. So now, let's go to pitching.

When you go to pitching, who's a better pitcher than Sandy Koufax or Bob Gibson or, right on down the line, Don Drysdale. And in our league, we had Satchel Paige, Smokey Joe Williams, Raymond Brown. So, you know, it's tough to compare eras. You have to; I guess each era produces its very best. So what I'm saying is that all these men, even the players today, if you are an All-Star today, most of the guys that became All-Stars could have played back in what we call the good old days. But we didn't name a manager. Again, Durocher is the best manager I have ever seen. When I say, for managing on the field, wanting to win. I only played for a couple managers and that was Leo Durocher, and Stan Hack when I played for the Cubs. And in the Negro Leagues, we had a man by the name of C. I. Taylor who was a great manager. So it is very, very difficult to say that this one is better than that one. It is tough to compare eras.

Now, I have a name. I failed to mention men like Martin Dihigo, a great Cuban pitcher. Real legend in Mexico and Cuba; in Cuba they have a big statue. He was the best I have ever seen. Nobody knows anything about him. They do down there, but he was a terrific ballplayer. I didn't mention Roberto Clemente. Look at what a great ballplayer he was. I haven't mentioned Mickey Mantle. Who is a much better player than Mickey? Mickey could run, hit, throw. He could do it all, run like a deer, great hitter and all. There were so many great, great players.

Stan Musial was the best left-hand hitter that I've ever seen. I played against him from '49 to '56. Never saw a better hitter than Stan Musial. I never saw Stan look bad. You would strike him out

Stan Musial

once in a while, but you never saw him look ridiculous at the plate. He came very, very close to hitting 500 home runs, but he was a line drive hitter. And one of the best ever, so again, there was so many good ones.

The best pitcher I ever hit against in the Negro Leagues, of course, was Paige. But there was a pitcher in the Nationals who played for the Cincinnati Reds. His name was Ewell Blackwell. Ewell Blackwell used to come up from the side, you know, and threw the ball from the side. And by the time you pick the ball up, he was almost upon you. Very, very tough. Very, very tough on me and almost everybody I would think. And then you have Warren Spahn. Spahn's a left-hander who won all those games.

Everything that I have is a result of playing baseball. It taught me to be competitive, to hang in there. It was almost a game I would have played for nothing. Most of the time I did play for almost nothing. And it gave me certain values that have taken me right through life. Learn how to play hard and play fair. Give it all you have. Be steadfast. It's just been a wonderful life. My kids grew up liking baseball and are still baseball fans. And I say it is the greatest game ever invented. So many things can happen, you play until somebody wins. You don't have a time clock and so on. First man up can get a hit. And there may be not another hit in the whole game, all kind of situations.

INDEX